How to Start Mastering the Digital Canvas

A Journey into Web3 Design

AF881099

Written by

RuPaul Getty

MetaReporter

MetaCouture

Artwork by

metaCOUTURE

MetaCouture

Credits

Written: January 3, 2024

Written by

RuPaul Getty

MetaReporter

MetaCouture

Artwork by

MetaCouture 2024

All Rights Reserved 2024

This book was written in association with MetaCouture by and with RuPaul Getty, the world's first transgender MetaReporter and Style MetaReporter of MetaCouture and in association with some AI elements. All Rights are Reserved by MetaCouture 2024.

Contents

1 Introduction to Digital Design

1.1 Understanding the Role of a Digital Designer

In today's digital age, the role of a digital designer has become increasingly important. With the rapid advancement of technology and the rise of the internet, the demand for skilled professionals who can create visually appealing and user-friendly digital experiences has grown exponentially. As we enter the world of Web3, where blockchain technology and decentralized applications (DApps) are transforming the way we interact with the internet, the role of a digital designer becomes even more crucial.

1.1,1 The Evolution of Digital Design

Before we delve into the specifics of the role of a digital designer in the Web3 era, it is essential to understand the evolution of digital design. Digital design encompasses a wide range of disciplines, including graphic design, user interface (UI) design, user experience (UX) design, and web design. Over the years, digital design has evolved from static web pages to dynamic and interactive experiences.

In the early days of the internet, web design primarily focused on creating visually appealing websites that provided information to users. However, with the advent of Web2, which introduced user-generated content and interactive web applications, the role of a digital designer expanded to include creating engaging and intuitive user experiences.

1.1.2 The Role of a Digital Designer

A digital designer is responsible for creating visually appealing and functional digital experiences. They combine their artistic skills with technical knowledge to design websites, mobile applications, and other digital interfaces. The role of a digital designer involves understanding user needs, creating wireframes and prototypes, selecting appropriate colors and typography, and ensuring a seamless user experience.

In the context of Web3, the role of a digital designer extends beyond traditional web and mobile design. Web3 introduces decentralized technologies, such as blockchain and smart contracts, which require a deep understanding of these concepts to design effective user interfaces for decentralized applications (DApps) and blockchain interactions.

1.1.3 Skills for Digital Designers in Web3

To become a successful digital designer in the world of Web3, it is essential to acquire a diverse set of skills. Here are some key skills that digital designers should focus on developing:

1. Technical Skills:

- Proficiency in design tools such as Adobe Creative Suite, Sketch, Figma, or other industry-standard software.
- Knowledge of HTML, CSS, and JavaScript to create interactive prototypes and collaborate effectively with developers.
- Familiarity with Web3 technologies, including blockchain, smart contracts, and decentralized applications.

2. Design Skills:

- Understanding of visual design principles, including layout, typography, color theory, and composition.
- Ability to create visually appealing and user-friendly interfaces that align with the brand identity and project goals.
- Knowledge of user experience (UX) design principles to ensure a seamless and intuitive user journey.

3. Communication and Collaboration Skills:

- Strong communication skills to effectively convey design ideas and collaborate with cross-functional teams, including developers, blockchain experts, and project stakeholders.
- Ability to receive and incorporate feedback to iterate and improve designs.
- Understanding of design thinking methodologies to approach problem-solving and user-centered design.

4. Adaptability and Continuous Learning:

- Willingness to adapt to new technologies and trends in the rapidly evolving Web3 landscape.
- Commitment to continuous learning and staying updated with the latest design tools, techniques, and best practices.

1.1.4 Tools for Digital Designers in Web3

In addition to the skills mentioned above, digital designers in the Web3 era should familiarize themselves with the tools and platforms specific to this domain. Here are some essential tools for Web3 design:

1. Blockchain Platforms:

- Ethereum: The most widely used blockchain platform for building decentralized applications (DApps) and smart contracts.

- Solana: A high-performance blockchain platform known for its scalability and speed.
- Polkadot: A multi-chain platform that enables interoperability between different blockchains.

2. Web3 Design Tools:

- Framer: A design tool that allows designers to create interactive prototypes for Web3 interfaces.
- MetaMask: A browser extension that enables users to interact with decentralized applications (DApps) and manage their blockchain assets.
- Remix: An integrated development environment (IDE) for writing, testing, and deploying smart contracts.

3. Collaboration and Workflow Tools:

- GitHub: A version control platform that facilitates collaboration between designers and developers.
- Zeplin: A design handoff tool that streamlines the process of sharing design assets and specifications with developers.
- Notion: A collaborative workspace that allows teams to organize and document their design processes.

By acquiring the necessary skills and familiarizing themselves with the tools and platforms specific to Web3 design, aspiring digital designers can enter the world of Web3 and contribute to the creation of innovative and user-centric digital experiences. The journey into

Web3 design is an exciting one, filled with opportunities for growth and creativity.

1.2 Exploring the Evolution of Web Design

Web design has come a long way since its inception. From simple static websites to dynamic and interactive web applications, the evolution of web design has been driven by advancements in technology and the changing needs and expectations of users. In this section, we will explore the journey of web design and how it has paved the way for the emergence of Web3.

1.2.1 The Early Days of Web Design

In the early days of the internet, web design was primarily focused on creating static websites with basic HTML and CSS. These websites were mainly used to provide information and had limited interactivity. Designers had to work within the constraints of slow internet connections and limited browser capabilities.

As technology advanced, web design started to incorporate more dynamic elements. The introduction of JavaScript allowed for the creation of interactive features such as image sliders, dropdown menus, and form validations. This marked the beginning of a more engaging and user-friendly web experience.

1.2.2 The Rise of Web 2.0

The term "Web 2.0" was coined to describe the shift from static websites to dynamic and collaborative platforms. With the advent of social media, online communities, and user-generated content, web design took on a whole new dimension. Websites became more interactive, allowing users to contribute, share, and collaborate.

During this period, the focus of web design shifted towards creating intuitive user interfaces and seamless user experiences. Designers started incorporating principles of visual design, typography, and color theory to enhance the aesthetics and usability of websites. The rise of responsive design also became crucial as websites needed to adapt to different screen sizes and devices.

1.2.3 The Birth of Web3

Web3 represents the next phase in the evolution of the internet. It is characterized by the integration of blockchain technology and decentralized applications (DApps) into web design. Web3 aims to empower users by giving them control over their data, enabling peer-to-peer transactions, and fostering trust and transparency.

With Web3, designers have the opportunity to create immersive and engaging experiences that leverage the power of blockchain technology. This includes designing user interfaces for DApps, creating digital collectibles (NFTs), and exploring new ways of interacting with the web.

1.2.4 The Impact of Web3 on Design

Web3 has brought about significant changes in the way designers approach their work. It has introduced new concepts and challenges that require a deep understanding of blockchain technology and its implications for design.

Designers working in the Web3 space need to consider factors such as security, privacy, and decentralization. They must also be familiar with smart contracts, blockchain protocols, and web3 frameworks and libraries. This knowledge allows them to design interfaces that provide a seamless and secure user experience.

Furthermore, Web3 design goes beyond aesthetics and usability. It involves designing for trust, transparency, and inclusivity. Designers must consider the ethical implications of their work and ensure that their designs align with the values of the Web3 community.

1.2.5 The Future of Web3 Design

As Web3 continues to evolve, the role of designers will become even more critical. Designers will need to stay updated with the latest advancements in blockchain technology, user experience design, and emerging trends in the Web3 space.

The future of Web3 design holds exciting possibilities. With the integration of artificial intelligence and machine learning, designers can create personalized and adaptive experiences. Virtual reality and augmented reality will also play a significant role in shaping the future of Web3 design, offering immersive and interactive experiences.

In conclusion, the evolution of web design has led us to the era of Web3, where blockchain technology and decentralized applications are transforming the way we interact with the internet. Aspiring digital designers can enter the world of Web3 by acquiring the necessary skills and knowledge in blockchain technology, user experience design, and emerging trends. By embracing the principles of Web3 design, designers can shape the future of the internet and create meaningful and impactful experiences for users.

1.3 Introduction to Web3 and its Impact on Design

In recent years, the digital landscape has undergone a significant transformation with the emergence of Web3 technologies. Web3, also known as the decentralized web, is a new paradigm that aims to revolutionize the way we interact with the internet. As a digital designer, understanding the fundamentals of Web3 and its impact on design is crucial to stay relevant in this rapidly evolving field.

1.3.1 What is Web3?

Web3 refers to the next generation of the internet, built on decentralized technologies such as blockchain. Unlike the traditional Web2, where centralized entities control and manage user data, Web3 aims to empower individuals by giving them control over their own data and digital assets. It enables peer-to-peer interactions, eliminates intermediaries, and fosters trust through transparency and immutability.

At the core of Web3 lies blockchain technology, a distributed ledger that records transactions across multiple computers. This technology ensures the integrity and security of data, making it tamper-proof and resistant to censorship. By leveraging blockchain, Web3 applications can provide users with unprecedented levels of privacy, security, and ownership.

1.3.2 The Impact of Web3 on Design

Web3 has a profound impact on the field of digital design, introducing new challenges and opportunities. Designers need to adapt their skills and mindset to create user-centric experiences in this decentralized ecosystem. Here are some key ways in which Web3 influences design:

1.3.2.1 User Empowerment and Ownership

Web3 puts users in control of their data and digital assets. This shift in ownership requires designers to consider new ways of designing interfaces that empower users to manage their information effectively. Designers must prioritize user privacy, security, and provide intuitive tools for users to interact with their digital assets.

1.3.2.2 Trust and Transparency

Blockchain technology, the backbone of Web3, ensures trust and transparency in transactions. Designers must communicate these principles through their designs, making it clear to users how their data is being used and ensuring transparency in the processes. Design elements such as visual cues, clear notifications, and user-friendly dashboards can help build trust in Web3 applications.

1.3.2.3 Seamless User Experience

Web3 applications often involve complex interactions with blockchain networks and decentralized protocols. Designers must strive to create seamless user experiences that abstract away the technical complexities. This requires a deep understanding of the underlying technologies and the ability to simplify complex concepts into intuitive interfaces.

1.3.2.4 Gamification and Incentives

Web3 introduces the concept of tokenization and incentivization through cryptocurrencies and non-fungible tokens (NFTs). Designers can leverage these elements to create engaging experiences that reward users for their participation. Gamification techniques, such as badges, leaderboards, and token rewards, can enhance user engagement and drive adoption.

1.3.2.5 Collaborative Design and Open Source

Web3 promotes collaboration and open-source development. Designers can contribute to the Web3 ecosystem by sharing their design assets, patterns, and best practices. Collaborative design tools and platforms enable designers to work together with developers, blockchain experts, and the community to create innovative and inclusive solutions.

1.3.3 Skills for Web3 Designers

To become a successful Web3 designer, you need to acquire a diverse set of skills that go beyond traditional digital design. Here are some essential skills and tools for Web3 designers:

1.3.3.1 Understanding Blockchain Technology

A solid understanding of blockchain technology is crucial for Web3 designers. Familiarize yourself with the fundamentals of blockchain, smart contracts, decentralized applications (DApps), and the principles of decentralization. This knowledge will help you design interfaces that align with the underlying technology.

1.3.3.2 User-Centric Design Thinking

Design thinking is a problem-solving approach that focuses on understanding user needs and creating solutions that meet those needs. Apply user-centric design thinking principles to create intuitive and engaging experiences in the Web3 space. Conduct user research, create user personas, and iterate on your designs based on user feedback.

1.3.3.3 Visual and Interaction Design

Strong visual and interaction design skills are essential for creating compelling Web3 interfaces. Develop a solid foundation in visual design principles, typography, color theory, and layout. Understand how to create intuitive navigation, microinteractions, and animations that enhance the user experience.

1.3.3.4 Prototyping and Wireframing

Prototyping and wireframing tools allow you to quickly iterate and test your design ideas. Familiarize yourself with tools like Figma, Sketch, or Adobe XD to create interactive prototypes that simulate the user experience. This will help you validate your design decisions and gather feedback from stakeholders and users.

1.3.3.5 Knowledge of Web3 Frameworks and Libraries

Web3 frameworks and libraries, such as Ethereum, IPFS, and Web3.js, are essential tools for building decentralized applications. While you may not need to code, having a basic understanding of these technologies will enable you to collaborate effectively with developers and make informed design decisions.

1.3.3.6 Continuous Learning and Adaptability

Web3 is a rapidly evolving field, and staying up-to-date with the latest trends and technologies is crucial. Embrace a mindset of continuous learning and adaptability. Engage with the Web3 community, attend conferences, and explore new design patterns and best practices to stay ahead in this dynamic industry.

By embracing the principles of Web3 and acquiring the necessary skills, you can position yourself as a valuable digital designer in the emerging world of decentralized applications and blockchain technology. The journey into Web3 design is an exciting one, filled with opportunities to shape the future of the internet and create meaningful experiences for users.

1.4 Skills and Tools for Digital Designers

As a digital designer looking to enter the world of Web3, it is essential to acquire a specific set of skills and familiarize yourself with the tools that will enable you to create innovative and engaging experiences. In this section, we will explore the key skills and tools that every digital designer should possess to thrive in the Web3 landscape.

1.4.1 Design Fundamentals

Before diving into the world of Web3, it is crucial to have a strong foundation in design principles and fundamentals. Understanding the principles of visual design, such as composition, balance, hierarchy, and color theory, will help you create aesthetically pleasing and visually impactful designs. Additionally, knowledge of typography and layout will enable you to effectively communicate information and create engaging user interfaces.

1.4.2 User Experience Design

User experience (UX) design plays a vital role in creating successful digital products. In the Web3 space, where decentralization and user empowerment are key, designing intuitive and seamless user experiences is even more critical. Familiarize yourself with UX design principles, such as user research, information architecture, wireframing, and prototyping. These skills will help you create user-centric designs that provide a smooth and enjoyable experience for Web3 users.

1.4.3 Web Design Tools

To bring your designs to life, you need to be proficient in using various design tools. Adobe Creative Suite, including Photoshop, Illustrator, and XD, is widely used in the design industry and offers a comprehensive set of tools for creating and editing visual assets. Sketch is another popular design tool among digital designers, known for its focus on user interface design. Figma, a cloud-based design tool, allows for collaborative design and prototyping, making it a valuable tool for Web3 projects.

1.4.4 Web3 Technologies and Concepts

To design for the Web3 ecosystem, it is essential to have a solid understanding of the underlying technologies and concepts. Familiarize yourself with blockchain technology, decentralized applications (DApps), and smart contracts. Learn about popular Web3 frameworks and libraries like Ethereum, Polkadot, and IPFS. Understanding these technologies will enable you to design interfaces that leverage the unique capabilities of Web3 and provide seamless interactions with blockchain networks.

1.4.5 Interaction Design and Animation

In the Web3 world, where user engagement is crucial, mastering interaction design and animation can take your designs to the next level. Learn how to create micro-interactions, transitions, and animations that enhance the user experience and provide visual feedback. Tools like Adobe After Effects, Principle, or Framer can help you prototype and animate your designs, allowing you to create immersive and engaging experiences for Web3 users.

1.4.6 Front-End Development

While not mandatory, having a basic understanding of front-end development can greatly benefit digital designers in the Web3 space. Knowing HTML, CSS, and JavaScript will enable you to communicate effectively with developers and understand the technical constraints and possibilities of your designs. Additionally, learning front-end frameworks like React or Vue.js can help you create interactive and dynamic user interfaces for Web3 applications.

1.4.7 Collaboration and Communication

Collaboration and communication skills are essential for digital designers working in the Web3 industry. As Web3 projects often involve cross-functional teams, being able to effectively communicate your design decisions and work collaboratively with developers, blockchain experts, and other stakeholders is crucial. Tools like Figma, InVision, or Zeplin can facilitate collaboration and streamline the design handoff process.

1.4.8 Continuous Learning and Adaptability

The world of Web3 is constantly evolving, with new technologies and trends emerging regularly. As a digital designer, it is essential to have a growth mindset and a willingness to continuously learn and adapt. Stay updated with the latest design trends, attend industry conferences and workshops, and engage with the Web3 community to expand your knowledge and stay ahead of the curve.

In conclusion, to become a digital designer in the Web3 space, you need to possess a strong foundation in design principles, user experience design, and interaction design. Familiarize yourself with the necessary design tools, such as Adobe Creative Suite, Sketch, and Figma. Gain a solid understanding of Web3 technologies and concepts, and consider learning front-end development to enhance your skill set. Additionally, cultivate collaboration and communication skills, and embrace continuous learning to thrive in the ever-evolving world of Web3 design.

2 Foundations of Web Design

2.1 Principles of Visual Design

Visual design is a fundamental aspect of digital design and plays a crucial role in creating engaging and effective user experiences. In this section, we will explore the principles of visual design that every digital designer should understand and apply when designing for the web3 environment.

2.1.1 Balance and Proportion

Balance and proportion are essential principles in visual design that help create a sense of harmony and equilibrium. Balance refers to the distribution of visual elements within a design, while proportion deals with the relative size and scale of these elements.

When designing for the web3, it is important to achieve a balanced composition that evenly distributes elements across the screen. This can be achieved through symmetrical or asymmetrical arrangements. Symmetrical balance creates a sense of stability and order, while asymmetrical balance adds visual interest and dynamism.

Proportion, on the other hand, ensures that the size and scale of elements are visually pleasing and coherent. It involves considering the relationship between different elements and their overall impact on the design. By maintaining proper proportion, you can create a visually appealing and well-structured design.

2.1.2 Contrast and Hierarchy

Contrast and hierarchy are crucial principles that help guide users' attention and create visual interest within a design. Contrast refers to the juxtaposition of different elements to create visual distinction and emphasis. It can be achieved through variations in color, size, shape, texture, or typography.

In web3 design, contrast can be used to highlight important elements such as call-to-action buttons, navigation menus, or key information. By using contrasting colors, sizes, or typography, you can draw users' attention to specific areas of the interface and guide them through the design.

Hierarchy, on the other hand, establishes the order of importance and organization within a design. It involves arranging elements in a way that clearly communicates their relative significance. By using visual cues such as size, color, or typography, you can create a clear hierarchy that guides users' understanding and interaction with the design.

2.1.3 Alignment and Grid Systems

Alignment and grid systems are essential tools for creating a visually cohesive and organized design. Alignment refers to the positioning of elements in relation to each other, while grid systems provide a framework for organizing content and maintaining consistency.

In web3 design, alignment helps create a sense of order and structure. By aligning elements along a common axis, you can establish visual connections and relationships between different parts of the design. This improves readability and makes the design more intuitive for users.

Grid systems, on the other hand, provide a framework for organizing content and maintaining consistency across different screens and devices. They help designers create layouts that are visually pleasing and easy to navigate. Grid systems also ensure that elements are properly spaced and aligned, enhancing the overall visual harmony of the design.

2.1.4 Color and Typography

Color and typography are powerful tools for creating visual impact and conveying meaning in digital design. They play a crucial role in establishing the overall mood and tone of a design, as well as enhancing readability and usability.

In web3 design, color can be used to evoke emotions, communicate brand identity, and differentiate elements within the interface. It is important to choose a color palette that aligns with the project's goals and target audience. Additionally, considering color accessibility guidelines is crucial to ensure that the design is inclusive and usable for all users.

Typography, on the other hand, involves the selection and arrangement of fonts to enhance readability and convey information effectively. In web3 design, typography should be legible and appropriate for the content being presented. It is important to consider factors such as font size, line spacing, and contrast to ensure optimal readability across different devices and screen sizes.

2.1.5 Visual Consistency and Branding

Visual consistency and branding are essential for creating a cohesive and memorable user experience. Consistency ensures that elements within a design are visually aligned and follow a set of established rules. It helps users navigate and understand the interface more easily.

In web3 design, consistency is particularly important due to the decentralized nature of the environment. Users should be able to recognize and understand the design patterns and visual cues across different decentralized applications (DApps) and websites. This can be achieved by establishing design guidelines and using consistent visual elements such as colors, typography, and icons.

Branding, on the other hand, involves creating a unique and recognizable identity for a web3 project or product. It encompasses the visual elements, messaging, and overall personality of the brand. By developing a strong brand identity, designers can create a sense of trust and familiarity among users, leading to increased engagement and loyalty.

In conclusion, understanding and applying the principles of visual design is crucial for digital designers looking to enter the world of web3. By mastering these principles, designers can create visually appealing and effective user experiences that align with the decentralized nature of the web3 environment.

2.2 Typography and Layout

Typography and layout are essential elements of web design that greatly influence the overall user experience. In this section, we will explore the importance of typography and layout in web design and how they can be effectively utilized to create visually appealing and user-friendly websites in the world of Web3.

2.2.1 The Power of Typography

Typography plays a crucial role in web design as it helps to convey information, set the tone, and create a visual hierarchy on a webpage. In the world of Web3, where user attention is limited and competition is fierce, using typography effectively can make a significant difference in capturing and retaining user engagement.

When choosing typography for your Web3 design, it is important to consider the following factors:

Readability and Legibility

The primary purpose of typography is to make the content readable and legible. Ensure that the chosen font is easy to read, even on different devices and screen sizes. Avoid using overly decorative or complex fonts that may hinder readability.

Consistency and Branding

Consistency in typography helps to establish a strong brand identity. Select a font or a combination of fonts that align with the brand's personality and values. Consistency in typography across different pages and sections of a website creates a cohesive and professional look.

Hierarchy and Emphasis

Typography can be used to create a visual hierarchy, guiding users through the content and highlighting important information. Use different font sizes, weights, and styles to differentiate headings, subheadings, and body text. This helps users quickly scan and understand the content structure.

Accessibility

Inclusive design is crucial in Web3, and typography plays a significant role in ensuring accessibility. Choose fonts that are accessible to users with visual impairments, and provide options for users to adjust font sizes and contrast settings.

2.2.2 Layout and Grid Systems

Layout is the arrangement of elements on a webpage, and it determines how users navigate and interact with the content. In Web3 design, a well-structured and intuitive layout is essential for creating a seamless user experience.

Grid Systems

Grid systems provide a framework for organizing content on a webpage. They help maintain consistency, balance, and alignment across different screen sizes and devices. Grid systems in Web3 design are particularly important as they ensure responsiveness and adaptability to various platforms.

Responsive Design

With the increasing use of mobile devices, responsive design has become a necessity in Web3. A responsive layout adjusts and adapts to different screen sizes, ensuring that the content is easily accessible and readable on any device. Utilize responsive design techniques such as fluid grids, flexible images, and media queries to create a seamless user experience across devices.

White Space

White space, also known as negative space, is the empty space between elements on a webpage. It helps to create visual breathing room, improve readability, and enhance the overall aesthetic appeal. In Web3 design, the strategic use of white space can help draw attention to important elements and create a sense of balance and harmony.

Visual Hierarchy

Layout plays a crucial role in establishing a visual hierarchy, guiding users through the content, and emphasizing key elements. Utilize techniques such as size, color, contrast, and positioning to create a clear and intuitive visual hierarchy. This ensures that users can easily navigate and understand the content structure.

2.2.3 Tools and Resources

To effectively utilize typography and layout in Web3 design, it is essential to leverage the right tools and resources. Here are some popular tools and resources that can assist you in creating visually appealing and user-friendly websites:

Typography Tools

- Google Fonts: A vast library of free and open-source fonts that can be easily integrated into web projects.
- Adobe Typekit: A subscription-based service that provides access to a wide range of high-quality fonts for web and print design.

- Font Pair: A website that suggests font pairings based on visual harmony and compatibility.

Layout Tools

- Figma: A collaborative design tool that allows for the creation of responsive layouts and the sharing of design assets.
- Sketch: A vector-based design tool that offers plugins and resources for creating responsive web layouts.
- Gridlover: A web-based tool that generates grid systems and typography scales based on user-defined parameters.

Online Resources

- Awwwards: A platform that showcases and recognizes outstanding web design, providing inspiration and insights into current design trends.
- Smashing Magazine: An online publication that offers articles, tutorials, and resources on web design, including typography and layout best practices.
- Dribbble: A community of designers that showcases their work, providing inspiration and insights into design techniques and trends.

By understanding the power of typography and layout and utilizing the right tools and resources, you can create visually stunning and user-friendly websites in the world of Web3. Remember to prioritize readability, consistency, accessibility, and responsiveness to ensure a seamless user experience across different devices and platforms.

2.3 Color Theory and Application

Color is a fundamental element of design that can greatly impact the overall look and feel of a website or digital product. In this section, we will explore the principles of color theory and how to effectively apply color in web design. Understanding color theory and its application is essential for digital designers looking to create visually appealing and engaging experiences in the world of Web3.

2.3.1 The Basics of Color Theory

Color theory is the study of how colors interact with each other and how they can be combined to create harmonious and visually pleasing compositions. By understanding the basic principles of color theory, digital designers can make informed decisions about color palettes and create designs that evoke the desired emotions and convey the intended message.

The Color Wheel

The color wheel is a visual representation of the relationships between colors. It consists of primary, secondary, and tertiary colors. Primary colors are the building blocks of all other colors and cannot be created by mixing other colors. Secondary colors are created by mixing two primary colors, while tertiary colors are created by mixing a primary color with a secondary color.

Color Harmony

Color harmony refers to the pleasing combination of colors in a design. There are various color harmonies that designers can use to create visually balanced and aesthetically pleasing compositions. Some common color harmonies include:

- Analogous: This harmony involves using colors that are adjacent to each other on the color wheel. It creates a sense of unity and is often used to create a calming and harmonious effect.
- Complementary: Complementary colors are opposite each other on the color wheel. They create a high contrast and vibrant effect when used together. This harmony is often used to draw attention and create visual impact.
- Triadic: Triadic harmony involves using three colors that are evenly spaced around the color wheel. It creates a balanced and dynamic composition.
- Monochromatic: Monochromatic harmony involves using different shades, tints, and tones of a single color. It creates a cohesive and harmonious look.

Color Psychology

Colors have the power to evoke emotions and influence human behavior. Understanding color psychology can help digital designers choose the right colors to convey the desired message and create the intended user experience. Here are some common associations with colors:

- Red: It is associated with energy, passion, and urgency. It can be used to create a sense of excitement or draw attention.
- Blue: Blue is often associated with trust, calmness, and reliability. It is commonly used in corporate and professional designs.
- Yellow: Yellow is associated with happiness, optimism, and creativity. It can be used to create a cheerful and uplifting atmosphere.
- Green: Green is associated with nature, growth, and harmony. It is often used in designs related to sustainability or health.
- Purple: Purple is associated with luxury, creativity, and spirituality. It can be used to create a sense of elegance and sophistication.
- Orange: Orange is associated with enthusiasm, warmth, and vitality. It can be used to create a sense of excitement and enthusiasm.

2.3.2 Applying Color in Web Design

Now that we have a basic understanding of color theory, let's explore how to effectively apply color in web design. Here are some key considerations:

Consistency and Branding

Consistency is crucial in web design, and color plays a significant role in establishing a consistent visual identity. When designing for

Web3, it is important to consider the branding and identity of the project or product. Use the brand's color palette consistently throughout the design to create a cohesive and recognizable experience for users.

Contrast and Readability

Color contrast is essential for ensuring readability and accessibility in web design. When choosing colors for text and background, make sure there is enough contrast to ensure that the text is easily readable. Consider factors such as color blindness and visual impairments when selecting colors to ensure inclusivity.

Visual Hierarchy

Color can be used to create a visual hierarchy and guide users' attention to important elements on a webpage. By using color strategically, designers can draw attention to call-to-action buttons, important information, or interactive elements. Consider using brighter or contrasting colors for elements that require immediate attention.

Mood and Emotion

Colors have the power to evoke specific moods and emotions. When designing for Web3, consider the desired mood or emotion you want to convey to users. For example, if you want to create a sense of trust and reliability, you might use a blue color palette. If you want to create a sense of excitement and energy, you might use a combination of red and orange.

Testing and Iteration

As with any design element, it is important to test and iterate on color choices. Conduct user testing to gather feedback on how users perceive and interact with the colors in your design. Make adjustments based on the feedback received to ensure that the chosen colors effectively communicate the desired message and create a positive user experience.

In conclusion, color theory and its application are essential skills for digital designers entering the world of Web3. By understanding the principles of color theory and applying them effectively in web design, designers can create visually appealing and engaging experiences that resonate with users. Consistency, contrast, visual hierarchy, mood, and emotion are all important considerations when working with color in web design. Remember to test and iterate on color choices to ensure that they align with the project's goals and create a positive user experience.

2.4 User Experience Design

User Experience (UX) design plays a crucial role in creating successful digital products and services. In the context of Web3, where decentralized applications and blockchain technology are at the forefront, UX design becomes even more important. In this section, we will explore the principles and practices of User Experience Design in the Web3 landscape.

2.4.1 Understanding User Experience Design

User Experience Design focuses on creating meaningful and enjoyable experiences for users when interacting with digital products. It involves understanding user needs, behaviors, and motivations to design intuitive and user-friendly interfaces. In the context of Web3, UX design encompasses not only the visual aspects but also the interactions and experiences related to blockchain technology and decentralized applications.

2.4.2 User-Centered Design Approach

A user-centered design approach is essential for creating successful Web3 experiences. It involves putting the user at the center of the design process and considering their needs, goals, and expectations. Here are some key steps to follow:

1. Research: Conduct user research to understand the target audience, their behaviors, and pain points. This can involve interviews, surveys, and usability testing.
2. User Personas: Create user personas to represent different types of users and their characteristics. This helps in designing for specific user needs and preferences.
3. User Flows: Map out user flows to understand the journey users will take when interacting with the Web3 application. Identify potential pain points and areas for improvement.

4. Information Architecture: Develop a clear and organized structure for the application, ensuring that information is easily accessible and understandable.
5. Wireframing and Prototyping: Create low-fidelity wireframes and interactive prototypes to visualize the user interface and test the usability of the design.
6. Usability Testing: Conduct usability testing with real users to gather feedback and identify areas of improvement. Iterate on the design based on the test results.
7. Visual Design: Apply visual design principles to create an aesthetically pleasing and cohesive interface. Consider the branding and visual identity of the Web3 project.
8. Interaction Design: Design intuitive and seamless interactions that guide users through the application. Consider the unique interactions and features of Web3 technologies.

2.4.3 Designing for Trust and Transparency

Web3 technologies, such as blockchain, are built on the principles of trust and transparency. As a UX designer, it is important to consider these principles when designing for Web3. Here are some key considerations:

1. Clear Information: Provide clear and concise information about the application's functionality, data ownership, and

security measures. Users should have a clear understanding of how their data is being used and protected.

2. Permission Requests: When requesting permissions or access to user data, provide clear explanations and options for users to control their data. Transparency and user control are crucial in building trust.
3. Security Measures: Design interfaces that prioritize security and privacy. Use encryption, two-factor authentication, and other security measures to protect user data and transactions.
4. Blockchain Feedback: Leverage the transparency of blockchain technology to provide users with real-time feedback on their transactions. This can include transaction confirmations, timestamps, and other relevant information.

2.4.4 Seamlessly Integrating Blockchain Interactions

In Web3 applications, users often interact with blockchain technology directly. As a UX designer, it is important to design seamless and intuitive interactions that bridge the gap between traditional web experiences and blockchain interactions. Here are some considerations:

1. Wallet Integration: Design interfaces that seamlessly integrate with cryptocurrency wallets. Provide clear instructions and guidance on how to connect wallets and manage transactions.

2. Transaction Feedback: Provide real-time feedback on transaction status and progress. Users should be able to track their transactions and understand the current state of their interactions with the blockchain.
3. Gas Fees: Clearly communicate gas fees and transaction costs to users. Consider providing estimates and options to optimize transaction costs.
4. Error Handling: Design error messages and notifications that are informative and actionable. Help users understand and resolve any issues that may arise during blockchain interactions.

2.4.5 Iterative Design and Continuous Improvement

Web3 technologies are constantly evolving, and user needs and expectations are ever-changing. Therefore, it is crucial to adopt an iterative design approach and continuously improve the user experience. Here are some strategies:

1. User Feedback: Actively seek feedback from users and the Web3 community. Engage in user testing, surveys, and feedback loops to gather insights and identify areas for improvement.
2. Analytics and Data: Utilize analytics tools to gather data on user behavior and interactions. Analyze this data to identify patterns, pain points, and opportunities for optimization.

3. Community Involvement: Engage with the Web3 community and gather insights from blockchain experts and developers. Collaborate with the community to understand emerging trends and best practices.

4. A/B Testing: Conduct A/B testing to compare different design variations and determine which performs better in terms of user engagement and satisfaction.

By following these principles and practices of User Experience Design, you can create engaging and user-friendly Web3 experiences that meet the needs and expectations of your target audience. Remember to continuously iterate and improve your designs based on user feedback and emerging trends in the Web3 landscape.

3. Web3 Technologies and Concepts

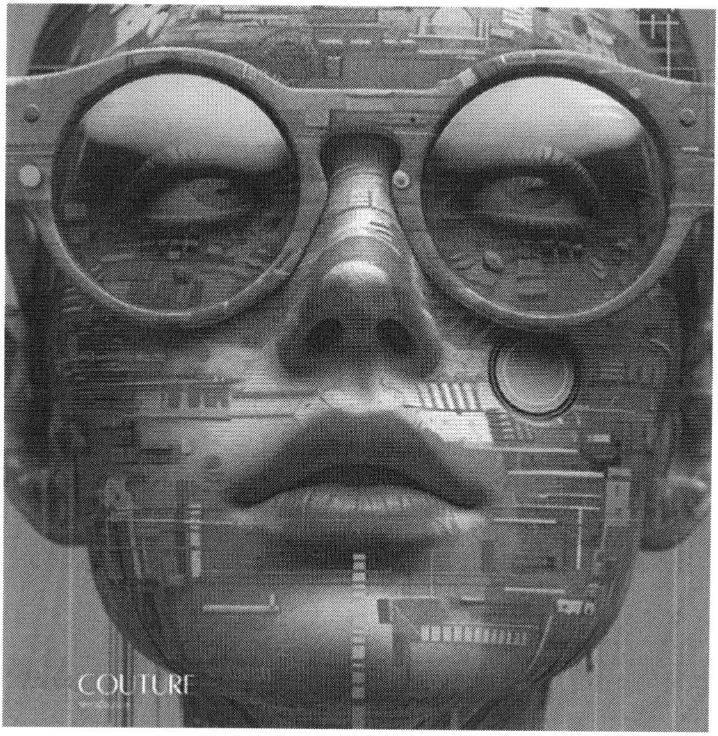

3.1. What is Blockchain?

Blockchain is a decentralized and distributed ledger technology that allows for secure and transparent transactions and interactions. It is essentially a chain of blocks, where each block contains a list of transactions or data. These blocks are linked together using cryptographic hashes, creating an immutable and tamper-proof record of all transactions.

The decentralized nature of blockchain means that there is no central authority or intermediary controlling the network. Instead, transactions are verified and recorded by a network of computers, known as nodes, which work together to maintain the integrity of the blockchain.

3.1.2 Key Principles of Blockchain Technology

3.1.2.1 Decentralization

Decentralization is one of the fundamental principles of blockchain technology. Unlike traditional centralized systems, where a single entity controls the data and transactions, blockchain distributes the control and ownership among multiple participants. This decentralization ensures transparency, security, and resilience of the network.

3.1.2.2 Transparency

Blockchain provides a transparent and auditable record of all transactions. Every transaction is recorded on the blockchain and can be viewed by anyone with access to the network. This transparency eliminates the need for trust in intermediaries and allows for greater accountability.

3.1.2.3 Security

Blockchain technology ensures the security of transactions through cryptographic algorithms. Each transaction is encrypted and linked to the previous transaction using a unique hash. This makes it extremely difficult for malicious actors to alter or tamper with the data stored on the blockchain.

3.1.2.4 Immutability

Once a transaction is recorded on the blockchain, it becomes immutable and cannot be altered or deleted. This immutability ensures the integrity of the data and provides a reliable and tamper-proof record of all transactions.

3.1.3 Types of Blockchains

There are primarily two types of blockchains: public and private.

3.1.3.1 Public Blockchains

Public blockchains, such as Bitcoin and Ethereum, are open to anyone and allow for anyone to participate in the network. These blockchains are maintained by a decentralized network of nodes, and transactions are verified through a consensus mechanism, such as Proof of Work (PoW) or Proof of Stake (PoS). Public blockchains are transparent, secure, and resistant to censorship.

3.1.3.2 Private Blockchains

Private blockchains, on the other hand, are restricted to a specific group of participants. These blockchains are often used by organizations or consortiums to streamline their internal processes and improve efficiency. Private blockchains offer more control and privacy compared to public blockchains but sacrifice some of the decentralization and transparency.

3.1.4 Applications of Blockchain Technology

Blockchain technology has a wide range of applications beyond cryptocurrencies. Here are a few examples:

3.1.4.1 Decentralized Finance (DeFi)

DeFi refers to the use of blockchain technology to recreate traditional financial systems in a decentralized manner. It enables peer-to-peer lending, decentralized exchanges, and other financial services without the need for intermediaries like banks. DeFi has the potential to revolutionize the financial industry by providing greater accessibility, transparency, and efficiency.

3.1.4.2 Supply Chain Management

Blockchain can be used to create transparent and traceable supply chains. By recording every step of the supply chain on the blockchain, companies can ensure the authenticity and provenance of their products. This can help in reducing fraud, improving efficiency, and enhancing consumer trust.

3.1.4.3 Identity Management

Blockchain technology can provide a secure and decentralized solution for identity management. By storing identity information on the blockchain, individuals can have greater control over their personal data and reduce the risk of identity theft. Blockchain-based identity systems can also streamline processes like KYC (Know Your Customer) and reduce the need for repetitive verification.

3.1.5 Design Considerations for Blockchain Applications

When designing for blockchain applications, there are several considerations that digital designers should keep in mind:

3.1.5.1 User Experience

Designers need to create intuitive and user-friendly interfaces for blockchain applications. Since blockchain technology can be complex for the average user, it is important to simplify the user experience and guide users through the process of interacting with the blockchain.

3.1.5.2 Visual Design

Visual design plays a crucial role in creating a cohesive and engaging user experience. Designers should consider the branding, typography, color palette, and overall aesthetics of the application to create a visually appealing interface that aligns with the values and goals of the blockchain project.

3.1.5.3 Security

Security is of utmost importance in blockchain applications. Designers should ensure that the application incorporates robust security measures, such as encryption and multi-factor authentication, to protect user data and transactions.

3.1.5.4 Scalability

Blockchain technology is still evolving, and scalability remains a challenge. Designers should consider the potential growth of the application and design interfaces that can accommodate a large number of users and transactions without compromising performance.

In conclusion, understanding blockchain technology is essential for digital designers looking to enter the world of Web3. By grasping the key principles and applications of blockchain, designers can create user-friendly and visually appealing interfaces that leverage the power of decentralized technology.

3.2 Decentralized Applications (DApps)

Decentralized Applications, commonly known as DApps, are one of the key components of the Web3 ecosystem. These applications leverage blockchain technology to provide users with a decentralized and transparent experience. In this section, we will explore the concept of DApps, their characteristics, and their significance in the world of Web3.

3.2.1 Understanding DApps

A DApp is an application that operates on a decentralized network, typically a blockchain. Unlike traditional applications that are hosted on centralized servers, DApps are built on top of blockchain platforms such as Ethereum, Polkadot, or Solana. This decentralized nature ensures that DApps are not controlled by any single entity, making them resistant to censorship and providing users with greater control over their data and digital assets.

DApps are designed to be open-source, meaning that their code is publicly available for anyone to inspect, modify, and contribute to. This transparency fosters trust among users and allows for community-driven development and innovation. Additionally, DApps often utilize smart contracts, which are self-executing contracts with the terms of the agreement directly written into code. Smart contracts enable automated and trustless interactions between users, eliminating the need for intermediaries.

3.2.2 Characteristics of DApps

DApps possess several key characteristics that distinguish them from traditional applications:

1. **Decentralization:** DApps operate on a decentralized network, ensuring that no single entity has control over the application or its data. This decentralization enhances security, transparency, and user autonomy.
2. **Open-source:** DApps are built using open-source code, allowing developers to contribute, audit, and improve the application. This collaborative approach fosters innovation and ensures the integrity of the application.
3. **Immutability:** Once deployed on the blockchain, DApps are immutable, meaning that their code and data cannot be altered or tampered with. This immutability ensures the integrity and trustworthiness of the application.
4. **Interoperability:** DApps can interact with other DApps and blockchain protocols, enabling seamless integration and

interoperability between different applications. This interoperability expands the functionality and potential use cases of DApps.

5. **Tokenization:** Many DApps utilize tokens as a means of value exchange within the application. These tokens can represent ownership rights, access to certain features, or even serve as a medium of exchange within the DApp ecosystem.

3.2.3 Types of DApps

DApps can be categorized into three main types based on their functionality and purpose:

1. **Financial DApps:** These DApps focus on providing decentralized financial services such as lending, borrowing, decentralized exchanges, and asset management. Examples of financial DApps include decentralized exchanges like Uniswap, lending platforms like Aave, and stablecoin protocols like MakerDAO.
2. **Gaming DApps:** Gaming DApps leverage blockchain technology to introduce new gaming experiences, ownership of in-game assets, and play-to-earn models. These DApps enable players to truly own their in-game assets and trade them on decentralized marketplaces. Popular gaming DApps include Axie Infinity, CryptoKitties, and Decentraland.
3. **Utility DApps:** Utility DApps offer various utility services such as decentralized file storage, decentralized identity management, decentralized social media, and decentralized

governance. Examples of utility DApps include Filecoin for decentralized file storage, uPort for decentralized identity management, and Steemit for decentralized social media.

3.2.4 Designing for DApps

Designing for DApps requires a deep understanding of blockchain technology, user experience design, and the principles of Web3. Here are some key considerations when designing DApps:

1. **User Experience:** DApps should provide a seamless and intuitive user experience, ensuring that users can easily navigate the application and understand its functionalities. Clear and concise user interfaces, logical information architecture, and thoughtful user flows are essential for a positive user experience.
2. **Security:** Security is of utmost importance in the Web3 world. DApps should be designed with security best practices in mind, including secure key management, protection against phishing attacks, and secure transaction handling. Conducting thorough security audits and implementing robust security measures are crucial to protect user funds and data.
3. **Decentralization:** DApps should embrace the principles of decentralization in their design. This includes avoiding single points of failure, ensuring data transparency, and providing users with control over their digital assets. Designing for decentralization requires careful consideration of the

underlying blockchain infrastructure and the integration of decentralized protocols.

4. **Visual Design:** The visual design of a DApp should align with its purpose and target audience. It should reflect the brand identity, evoke trust, and provide a visually appealing experience. Consistency in typography, color palette, and layout is important to create a cohesive and engaging user interface.

5. **Accessibility:** DApps should be accessible to users of all abilities. Designers should consider accessibility guidelines and ensure that the application is usable by individuals with disabilities. This includes providing alternative text for images, using color contrasts that are readable for visually impaired users, and designing for keyboard navigation.

Designing for DApps requires a multidisciplinary approach, combining the principles of traditional design with the unique characteristics of Web3. By understanding the decentralized nature of DApps and considering the needs of the users, designers can create engaging and user-centric experiences within the Web3 ecosystem.

3.3 Smart Contracts and Solidity

Smart contracts are an integral part of the Web3 ecosystem, enabling decentralized applications (DApps) to function autonomously and securely. In this section, we will explore the concept of smart contracts and delve into Solidity, the programming language used to write them.

3.3.1 Understanding Smart Contracts

A smart contract is a self-executing contract with the terms of the agreement directly written into code. It automatically executes actions once predefined conditions are met, eliminating the need for intermediaries or third parties. Smart contracts are stored on a blockchain, ensuring transparency, immutability, and security.

Smart contracts have revolutionized various industries by enabling trustless transactions and automating complex processes. They have applications in finance, supply chain management, voting systems, and more. As a digital designer, understanding smart contracts is crucial to designing user interfaces and experiences for DApps.

3.3.2 Introducing Solidity

Solidity is a high-level programming language specifically designed for writing smart contracts on the Ethereum blockchain. It is statically typed, supports inheritance, and has similar syntax to JavaScript. Solidity allows developers to define the behavior of smart contracts, including their functions, variables, and events.

To become a proficient Web3 designer, it is essential to have a basic understanding of Solidity. While you may not need to write smart contracts yourself, having knowledge of the language will enable you to collaborate effectively with developers and understand the technical aspects of DApp design.

3.3.3 Solidity Basics

To get started with Solidity, it is helpful to familiarize yourself with some of its key concepts and syntax:

Contract Structure

A Solidity contract is defined using the contract keyword, followed by the contract name. It encapsulates the data and functions of the smart contract.

contract MyContract { // Contract code goes here}

State Variables

State variables store the data of the smart contract. They can be of various types, such as integers, strings, arrays, or custom-defined structs.

contract MyContract {uint public myNumber; // Public state variable string private myString; // Private state variable// ...}

Functions

Functions define the behavior of the smart contract. They can be called internally or externally, and can modify the state of the contract.

contract MyContract { uint public myNumber; function setNumber(uint _number) public { myNumber = _number; }

function getNumber() public view returns (uint) { return myNumber; }

Events

Events are used to communicate information from the smart contract to the outside world. They can be emitted within functions and can be listened to by external applications.

contract MyContract { event NumberSet(uint number);

function setNumber(uint _number) public { myNumber = _number; emit NumberSet(_number);}

Modifiers

Modifiers are used to modify the behavior of functions. They can be applied before or after a function is executed and are often used for access control or input validation.

contract MyContract { address public owner; modifier onlyOwner() { require(msg.sender == owner, "Only the owner can call this function"); _; } function changeOwner(address _newOwner) public onlyOwner { owner = _newOwner; }

3.3.4 Learning Solidity

To gain proficiency in Solidity, there are several resources available:

Online Tutorials and Courses

Numerous online tutorials and courses provide step-by-step guidance on learning Solidity. These resources cover the basics of the language, as well as more advanced topics such as contract testing and security considerations.

Solidity Documentation

The official Solidity documentation is an invaluable resource for understanding the language in-depth. It provides detailed explanations of each Solidity feature, along with code examples and best practices.

Community Forums and Developer Communities

Engaging with the Solidity community can be immensely helpful in learning the language. Participate in forums, join developer communities, and attend meetups or conferences to connect with experienced Solidity developers and gain insights from their experiences.

Conclusion

Smart contracts and Solidity are fundamental components of Web3 design. Understanding how smart contracts work and having a basic knowledge of Solidity will empower you as a digital designer to create intuitive and user-friendly interfaces for DApps. By collaborating effectively with developers and understanding the technical aspects of Web3, you can contribute to the creation of innovative and impactful decentralized applications.

3.4 Interacting with Web3 APIs

In the world of Web3, interacting with Web3 APIs is a crucial skill for digital designers. Web3 APIs allow designers to connect their designs with the underlying blockchain technology and decentralized applications (DApps). This interaction enables designers to create immersive and engaging user experiences that leverage the power of blockchain and smart contracts.

3.4.1 Understanding Web3 APIs

Web3 APIs, also known as blockchain APIs, are interfaces that allow designers to communicate with the blockchain network and access its functionalities. These APIs provide a set of methods and protocols that enable designers to interact with smart contracts, retrieve data from the blockchain, and perform various operations.

There are different types of Web3 APIs available, each serving a specific purpose. Some common Web3 APIs include:

1. **Ethereum API (Web3.js)**: This API is specifically designed for interacting with the Ethereum blockchain. It provides a wide range of functions to interact with smart contracts, send transactions, and retrieve data from the blockchain.

2. **IPFS API**: The InterPlanetary File System (IPFS) API allows designers to store and retrieve files on the decentralized IPFS network. It provides methods to upload files, retrieve their content, and manage the IPFS network.

3. **Oracles API**: Oracles are services that provide external data to smart contracts. Oracles APIs allow designers to fetch real-world data, such as price feeds, weather information, or any other external data, and integrate it into their DApps.

4. **Blockchain Explorer API**: Blockchain explorers provide a way to search and explore the blockchain. These APIs allow designers to retrieve transaction details, view account balances, and explore the history of the blockchain.

3.4.2 Integrating Web3 APIs into Design Workflows

To effectively integrate Web3 APIs into their design workflows, digital designers need to have a solid understanding of the underlying blockchain technology and the specific APIs they are working with. Here are some steps to help designers get started:

1. **Research and Familiarize**: Start by researching and familiarizing yourself with the blockchain platform you are designing for. Understand the core concepts, such as smart contracts, decentralized storage, and blockchain transactions. This knowledge will help you understand how the Web3 APIs work and how they can be integrated into your designs.

2. **Choose the Right API**: Depending on the requirements of your project, choose the appropriate Web3 API to work with. Consider factors such as the blockchain platform, the functionalities required, and the programming language you are comfortable with. For example, if you are designing for

Ethereum, you can use the Web3.js library to interact with the Ethereum blockchain.

3. **Set Up Development Environment**: Set up a development environment that allows you to test and interact with the Web3 API. This may involve installing the necessary software, such as a blockchain client or a development framework like Truffle, and configuring it to connect to the desired blockchain network.

4. **Learn the API Documentation**: Study the API documentation provided by the blockchain platform or library you are using. Understand the available methods, their parameters, and the expected outputs. This will help you design user interfaces that effectively communicate with the blockchain.

5. **Design User Interfaces**: Design user interfaces that enable users to interact with the blockchain functionalities seamlessly. Consider the specific actions users need to perform, such as sending transactions, interacting with smart contracts, or retrieving data from the blockchain. Ensure that the user interface is intuitive and provides clear feedback on the status of the blockchain operations.

6. **Prototype and Test**: Create prototypes of your designs and test them with real data from the blockchain. Use the Web3 API to simulate interactions and validate the user experience. This iterative process will help you refine your designs and identify any usability issues.

7. **Collaborate with Developers**: Collaborate closely with developers and blockchain experts to ensure the smooth integration of your designs with the Web3 APIs. Work together to address any technical challenges and ensure that the design and functionality align seamlessly.

3.4.3 Design Considerations for Web3 API Integration

When integrating Web3 APIs into your designs, there are several important considerations to keep in mind:

1. **Security**: Ensure that your designs follow best practices for security. Protect user data and transactions by implementing secure communication protocols and encryption techniques. Be aware of potential vulnerabilities and design with security in mind.

2. **Error Handling**: Design user interfaces that provide clear and informative error messages in case of failed transactions or other errors. Help users understand the reason for the error and guide them on how to resolve it.

3. **Performance**: Optimize your designs for performance by minimizing the number of API calls and optimizing data retrieval. Consider caching mechanisms and asynchronous loading to enhance the user experience.

4. **Scalability**: Design with scalability in mind, as blockchain networks can experience high traffic and congestion. Ensure that your designs can handle increased user activity and adapt to changing network conditions.

5. **User Education**: Educate users about the blockchain technology and the functionalities provided by the Web3 APIs. Provide clear instructions and guidance on how to interact with the blockchain through your designs.

By mastering the art of interacting with Web3 APIs, digital designers can unlock the full potential of Web3 technologies and create innovative and immersive user experiences. Embrace the opportunities that Web3 offers and continue to explore and experiment with the evolving landscape of blockchain and decentralized applications.

3.5 NFTs and Digital Collectibles

In recent years, the world of digital art and collectibles has been revolutionized by the emergence of Non-Fungible Tokens (NFTs). NFTs have gained significant attention and popularity, opening up new opportunities for digital designers in the realm of Web3. In this section, we will explore the concept of NFTs and digital collectibles, their impact on the design industry, and how you can leverage these technologies to enter the world of Web3 as a digital designer.

3.5.1 Understanding NFTs

Non-Fungible Tokens (NFTs) are unique digital assets that are stored on a blockchain, typically on platforms like Ethereum. Unlike cryptocurrencies such as Bitcoin or Ethereum, which are fungible and can be exchanged on a one-to-one basis, NFTs are indivisible and cannot be exchanged on a like-for-like basis. Each NFT has a distinct value and ownership, making it a one-of-a-kind digital item.

NFTs can represent various forms of digital content, including artwork, music, videos, virtual real estate, and even virtual goods within video games. These digital assets are tokenized, meaning they are assigned a unique token ID that verifies their authenticity and ownership. The ownership and transaction history of NFTs are recorded on the blockchain, providing transparency and immutability.

3.5.2 The Impact of NFTs on the Design Industry

The introduction of NFTs has had a profound impact on the design industry, particularly in the realm of digital art and collectibles. NFTs have created a new market for artists and designers to monetize their digital creations directly, without the need for intermediaries such as galleries or auction houses. This has democratized the art world, allowing artists to reach a global audience and receive fair compensation for their work.

As a digital designer, NFTs provide you with an opportunity to showcase your creativity and skills in a unique and innovative way. By creating and selling digital collectibles, you can establish yourself as a digital artist and build a reputation within the Web3 community. NFTs also enable you to explore new forms of expression and experimentation, pushing the boundaries of traditional design.

3.5.3 Creating NFTs as a Digital Designer

To enter the world of Web3 as a digital designer, you can start by creating your own NFTs. Here are some steps to get you started:

1. **Choose your medium**: Decide on the type of digital content you want to create as an NFT. It could be digital artwork, illustrations, animations, or even interactive experiences.
2. **Create your digital assets**: Utilize your design skills and tools to create high-quality digital assets. Pay attention to the resolution, format, and overall aesthetics of your creations.
3. **Choose a blockchain platform**: Select a blockchain platform that supports NFTs, such as Ethereum, Binance Smart Chain, or Flow. Each platform has its own ecosystem and marketplace for NFTs.
4. **Set up a digital wallet**: Create a digital wallet that is compatible with the blockchain platform you have chosen. This wallet will be used to store and manage your NFTs.
5. **Mint your NFTs**: Minting refers to the process of creating and tokenizing your digital assets as NFTs. This process typically involves paying a fee and following the platform's guidelines.
6. **List your NFTs for sale**: Once your NFTs are minted, you can list them for sale on various NFT marketplaces. These marketplaces act as platforms for buying, selling, and trading NFTs.

7. **Promote your NFTs**: Use social media, online communities, and other marketing channels to promote your NFTs and attract potential buyers. Engage with the Web3 community and collaborate with other artists and collectors.

By following these steps, you can establish yourself as a digital designer in the world of Web3 and start monetizing your creative work through NFTs.

3.5.4 Design Considerations for NFTs

When creating NFTs as a digital designer, there are several design considerations to keep in mind:

1. **Uniqueness and scarcity**: NFTs derive their value from their uniqueness and scarcity. Consider creating limited editions or one-of-a-kind pieces to increase the desirability of your NFTs.
2. **Metadata and token attributes**: Enhance the value of your NFTs by adding metadata and token attributes. This could include information about the artwork, the artist's statement, or even additional perks for the owner of the NFT.
3. **Presentation and packaging**: Pay attention to how you present and package your NFTs. Consider creating visually appealing thumbnails, descriptions, and accompanying media to attract potential buyers.
4. **Interactivity and utility**: Explore ways to make your NFTs interactive or provide utility to the owners. This could

involve embedding hidden messages, unlocking additional content, or granting access to exclusive events.

5. **Collaborations and partnerships**: Consider collaborating with other artists, musicians, or influencers to create unique and valuable NFT collections. Collaborations can help expand your reach and attract a wider audience.

By considering these design elements, you can create compelling and valuable NFTs that resonate with collectors and enthusiasts in the Web3 community.

Conclusion

NFTs and digital collectibles have opened up exciting opportunities for digital designers in the world of Web3. By understanding the concept of NFTs, their impact on the design industry, and how to create and market your own NFTs, you can enter this emerging field and establish yourself as a digital artist. Embrace the possibilities of Web3, push the boundaries of traditional design, and embark on a journey of creativity and innovation in the digital realm.

4 Designing for Web3

4.1 Designing User Interfaces for DApps

Designing user interfaces (UI) for decentralized applications (DApps) requires a unique set of skills and considerations. In this section, we will explore the key principles and best practices for creating intuitive and engaging UIs in the world of Web3.

4.1.1 Understanding the DApp Ecosystem

Before diving into the design process, it is crucial to understand the DApp ecosystem and its unique characteristics. Unlike traditional web applications, DApps are built on blockchain technology, which introduces new possibilities and constraints.

DApps are decentralized, meaning they operate on a peer-to-peer network without relying on a central authority. They leverage blockchain technology to ensure transparency, immutability, and security. As a digital designer, it is essential to grasp these fundamental concepts to create effective UIs.

4.1.2 User-Centric Design Approach

Just like designing for traditional web applications, a user-centric design approach is crucial when designing UIs for DApps. Understanding the target audience, their needs, and their goals is the foundation of creating a successful user experience.

Start by conducting user research to gain insights into the target users' preferences, behaviors, and pain points. This research will help you identify design opportunities and inform your decision-making process throughout the design phase.

4.1.3 Simplified Onboarding Process

One of the challenges in designing for DApps is the onboarding process. Unlike traditional applications, DApps often require users to interact with blockchain networks, which can be complex and unfamiliar to many users.

To overcome this challenge, focus on creating a simplified onboarding process that guides users through the necessary steps. Provide clear instructions, tooltips, and informative error messages to help users understand the actions they need to take.

Consider integrating wallet providers or browser extensions that simplify the process of connecting to the blockchain. This can help streamline the onboarding experience and reduce friction for users.

4.1.4 Intuitive Navigation and Information Architecture

Creating an intuitive navigation system and information architecture is crucial for DApp UI design. Users should be able to easily understand the structure of the application and navigate between different sections.

Consider using familiar design patterns and conventions to make the UI feel intuitive. Use clear and descriptive labels for navigation elements and organize content in a logical and hierarchical manner.

Additionally, leverage visual cues such as icons, color coding, and tooltips to provide users with contextual information and guide them through the application.

4.1.5 Responsive and Adaptive Design

Designing UIs for DApps requires considering various devices and screen sizes. Just like traditional web design, it is essential to create responsive and adaptive UIs that provide a consistent experience across different devices.

Ensure that the UI elements and layout adapt gracefully to different screen sizes. Use responsive design techniques such as fluid grids, flexible images, and media queries to optimize the UI for different devices.

4.1.6 Consistency and Branding

Consistency in UI design is crucial for creating a cohesive and memorable user experience. Establish a consistent visual language, including typography, color palette, and iconography, that aligns with the DApp's branding.

Maintain consistency in the placement and behavior of UI elements throughout the application. This will help users develop a mental model of the application and navigate it more efficiently.

4.1.7 Feedback and Microinteractions

Providing feedback and incorporating microinteractions into the UI can greatly enhance the user experience. Feedback helps users understand the outcome of their actions and provides reassurance that the system is responding.

Consider incorporating animations, transitions, and subtle visual cues to provide feedback and make the UI feel more responsive. For example, display loading indicators during network transactions or highlight selected elements to indicate user actions.

4.1.8 Security and Trust

Security is a critical aspect of designing UIs for DApps. Users need to trust the application with their sensitive information and assets. As a designer, you can contribute to building trust by incorporating security features into the UI.

Clearly communicate the security measures in place, such as encryption and multi-factor authentication. Use visual cues, such as lock icons or color indicators, to indicate secure connections or actions.

4.1.9 Usability Testing and Iteration

Usability testing is an essential part of the design process for DApp UIs. Conduct user testing sessions to gather feedback and identify areas for improvement. Iterate on the design based on the insights gained from user testing.

Consider involving users with varying levels of familiarity with blockchain technology to ensure that the UI is accessible to a wide range of users. Incorporate their feedback to refine the UI and enhance the overall user experience.

4.1.10 Collaborating with Developers

Collaboration between designers and developers is crucial for successful DApp UI design. Work closely with developers to understand the technical constraints and possibilities of the underlying blockchain technology.

Maintain open communication channels to ensure that the design vision is effectively translated into the final product. Collaborate on the implementation of UI components and animations to ensure a seamless user experience.

By following these principles and best practices, you can create user-friendly and visually appealing UIs for DApps. Embrace the unique opportunities and challenges of the Web3 world to design innovative and engaging experiences for users.

4.2 Creating Engaging Web3 Experiences

In the rapidly evolving world of web design, it is essential for digital designers to stay ahead of the curve and adapt to new technologies and trends. Web3, the next generation of the internet, is revolutionizing the way we interact with digital platforms and presents exciting opportunities for designers to create engaging and immersive experiences. In this section, we will explore the key principles and strategies for designing captivating Web3 experiences.

4.2.1 Understanding the Web3 Landscape

Before diving into the design process, it is crucial to have a solid understanding of the Web3 landscape. Web3 refers to the decentralized web, powered by blockchain technology and smart contracts. It enables peer-to-peer interactions, eliminates intermediaries, and provides users with greater control over their data and digital assets.

To become a successful Web3 designer, familiarize yourself with the underlying technologies such as blockchain, decentralized applications (DApps), smart contracts, and non-fungible tokens (NFTs). Stay updated with the latest advancements in Web3 frameworks and libraries, as they provide the building blocks for creating immersive experiences.

4.2.2 Designing for User Engagement

Creating engaging Web3 experiences requires a deep understanding of user behavior and psychology. Here are some strategies to consider:

4.2.2.1 Gamification and Incentives

Leverage gamification techniques to incentivize user participation and create a sense of achievement. Integrate reward systems, badges, and leaderboards to encourage users to explore and interact with your platform. Design visually appealing and meaningful NFTs that users can collect and trade, adding value to their experience.

4.2.2.2 Interactive and Immersive Elements

Engage users by incorporating interactive and immersive elements into your design. Utilize 3D graphics, animations, and virtual reality (VR) to create a captivating and memorable experience. Consider the use of sound effects and haptic feedback to enhance user engagement and create a multisensory experience.

4.2.2.3 Personalization and Customization

Empower users to personalize their experience by providing customization options. Allow them to choose themes, layouts, and color schemes that resonate with their preferences. Implement dynamic content that adapts to user behavior and preferences, creating a personalized and tailored experience.

4.2.3 Designing for Accessibility and Inclusivity

Inclusive design is a fundamental aspect of creating engaging Web3 experiences. Consider the following principles:

4.2.3.1 Universal Design

Adopt a universal design approach to ensure your platform is accessible to users with diverse abilities. Provide alternative text for images, captions for videos, and clear navigation for screen readers. Consider color contrast and font size to accommodate users with visual impairments.

4.2.3.2 Multilingual Support

Design your platform to support multiple languages, enabling users from different regions to access and engage with your content. Consider the cultural nuances and preferences of your target audience to create a truly inclusive experience.

4.2.3.3 Accessibility Testing

Conduct regular accessibility testing to identify and address any barriers that may hinder user engagement. Test your platform with assistive technologies and involve users with disabilities in the testing process to gain valuable insights and feedback.

4.2.4 Designing for Trust and Security

Trust and security are paramount in the Web3 ecosystem. Consider the following strategies to instill trust in your users:

4.2.4.1 Transparent Information Architecture

Design a clear and transparent information architecture that allows users to understand how their data is collected, stored, and used. Provide clear explanations of the security measures in place to protect user information and digital assets.

4.2.4.2 User Control and Ownership

Empower users by giving them control over their data and digital assets. Implement features that allow users to manage permissions, revoke access, and transfer ownership of their assets securely.

4.2.4.3 Secure User Onboarding

Design a seamless and secure onboarding process that instills confidence in users. Implement two-factor authentication, encryption, and other security measures to protect user accounts and prevent unauthorized access.

4.2.5 Iterative Design and User Feedback

Designing engaging Web3 experiences is an iterative process that requires continuous improvement based on user feedback. Consider the following strategies:

4.2.5.1 User Testing and Feedback

Conduct user testing sessions to gather feedback and insights on the usability and engagement of your platform. Incorporate user feedback into your design iterations to enhance the overall user experience.

4.2.5.2 Analytics and Data-driven Design

Leverage analytics tools to gather data on user behavior, engagement, and conversion rates. Analyze this data to identify areas for improvement and optimize your design decisions based on user preferences and needs.

4.2.5.3 A/B Testing

Implement A/B testing to compare different design variations and determine which performs better in terms of user engagement and conversion. Use the insights gained from A/B testing to refine your design and optimize user engagement.

By following these principles and strategies, you can create engaging Web3 experiences that captivate users and provide them with a seamless and immersive journey through the decentralized web. Embrace the evolving landscape of Web3 and continue to learn and adapt as new technologies and trends emerge.

4.3 Designing for Blockchain Interactions

Designing for blockchain interactions is a crucial aspect of web3 design. As blockchain technology continues to revolutionize various industries, including finance, supply chain, and gaming, it is essential for digital designers to understand how to create intuitive and user-friendly interfaces for blockchain-based applications. In this section, we will explore the key considerations and best practices for designing effective blockchain interactions.

4.3.1 Understanding Blockchain Interactions

Before diving into the design process, it is important to have a solid understanding of how blockchain interactions work. Blockchain technology is built on the principles of decentralization, transparency, and immutability. It allows users to interact with decentralized applications (DApps) and perform various actions, such as transferring assets, executing smart contracts, and participating in governance processes.

When designing for blockchain interactions, digital designers need to consider the unique characteristics of blockchain technology. These include:

4.3.1.1 Trust and Security

Blockchain technology eliminates the need for intermediaries by providing a trustless environment. Transactions and data stored on the blockchain are secured through cryptographic algorithms, ensuring the integrity and security of the system. Designers should prioritize creating interfaces that instill trust in users and clearly communicate the security measures in place.

4.3.1.2 Complexity and Technical Jargon

Blockchain technology can be complex, especially for users who are new to the space. Digital designers should strive to simplify the user experience and avoid overwhelming users with technical jargon. Clear and concise language, along with intuitive visual cues, can help users navigate through the application and understand the actions they are performing.

4.3.1.3 Transaction Confirmation and Feedback

Blockchain transactions often require multiple confirmations before they are considered final. Designers should provide clear feedback to users during the transaction process, indicating the status of their transactions and any necessary steps they need to take. Visual indicators, such as progress bars or notifications, can help users track the progress of their transactions and reduce anxiety.

4.3.2 Designing Intuitive User Interfaces

When designing user interfaces for blockchain interactions, it is important to prioritize usability and simplicity. Here are some best practices to consider:

4.3.2.1 Clear Navigation and Information Hierarchy

A well-structured and intuitive navigation system is crucial for users to easily find the information they need. Designers should carefully consider the information hierarchy and organize the interface in a logical manner. Clear labels, breadcrumbs, and menus can help users navigate through different sections of the application.

4.3.2.2 Consistent and Familiar Design Patterns

To provide a seamless user experience, designers should leverage familiar design patterns and conventions. Users are more likely to feel comfortable and confident when interacting with an interface that follows established design principles. However, it is also important to balance familiarity with innovation to create unique and engaging experiences.

4.3.2.3 Visualizing Blockchain Data

Blockchain applications often involve complex data structures and transactions. Designers should find creative ways to visualize this data in a clear and understandable manner. Infographics, charts, and graphs can help users comprehend complex information and make informed decisions.

4.3.2.4 Responsive and Mobile-Friendly Design

With the increasing use of mobile devices, it is crucial to design interfaces that are responsive and mobile-friendly. Users should be able to access and interact with blockchain applications seamlessly across different devices and screen sizes. Responsive design principles, such as flexible layouts and scalable typography, should be implemented to ensure a consistent experience.

4.3.3 Enhancing User Trust and Security

Building trust and ensuring the security of user interactions are paramount in blockchain design. Here are some considerations to keep in mind:

4.3.3.1 Onboarding and Education

Blockchain technology can be intimidating for new users. Designers should provide clear onboarding processes and educational resources to help users understand the benefits and risks of blockchain interactions. Tutorials, tooltips, and interactive guides can assist users in navigating the application and performing actions securely.

4.3.3.2 Visualizing Security Measures

To instill trust in users, designers should visually communicate the security measures in place. This can include displaying security badges, encryption icons, or other visual indicators that reassure users about the safety of their transactions and data.

4.3.3.3 Two-Factor Authentication (2FA)

Implementing two-factor authentication adds an extra layer of security to blockchain interactions. Designers should consider incorporating 2FA into the interface design and provide clear instructions on how to set it up and use it effectively.

4.3.4 Iterative Design and User Testing

As with any design process, iteration and user testing are crucial for creating effective blockchain interactions. Designers should gather feedback from users and iterate on the interface based on their needs and preferences. User testing can help identify pain points, usability issues, and areas for improvement.

By following these best practices and considering the unique characteristics of blockchain technology, digital designers can create intuitive and user-friendly interfaces for blockchain interactions. As the web3 ecosystem continues to evolve, designers will play a vital role in shaping the future of decentralized applications and enhancing the user experience in the blockchain space.

4.4 Designing NFTs and Digital Art

In the world of Web3, Non-Fungible Tokens (NFTs) have gained significant popularity. NFTs are unique digital assets that can represent ownership or proof of authenticity for various types of digital content, including artwork, music, videos, and more. As a digital designer, understanding how to design NFTs and digital art is crucial to stay relevant in this rapidly evolving landscape.

4.4.1 Understanding NFTs

Before diving into the design process, it's essential to have a solid understanding of what NFTs are and how they function. NFTs are built on blockchain technology, typically using Ethereum's blockchain. Each NFT has a unique identifier that distinguishes it from other tokens, making it indivisible and irreplaceable. This uniqueness is what gives NFTs their value and appeal.

NFTs can be used to represent various forms of digital art, such as illustrations, animations, 3D models, and even virtual reality experiences. These digital assets can be bought, sold, and traded on various NFT marketplaces, providing artists and creators with new opportunities to monetize their work.

4.4.2 Designing NFTs

Designing NFTs requires a combination of artistic skills and an understanding of the technical aspects of blockchain technology. Here are some key considerations to keep in mind when designing NFTs:

4.4.2.1 Concept and Storytelling

Just like any other form of art, NFTs should have a strong concept and tell a compelling story. Think about the message or emotion you want to convey through your artwork. Consider the themes, symbolism, and narrative elements that will resonate with your audience. NFT collectors are often drawn to pieces that have a deeper meaning or evoke a strong emotional response.

4.4.2.2 Visual Appeal and Aesthetics

The visual appeal of your NFT is crucial in attracting potential buyers and collectors. Pay attention to the composition, color palette, and overall aesthetics of your artwork. Experiment with different styles and techniques to create a unique and visually striking piece. Remember that NFTs are often displayed on digital platforms, so consider how your artwork will look in various digital environments.

4.4.2.3 Technical Specifications

When designing NFTs, it's important to adhere to the technical specifications required by the NFT marketplace or platform you plan to use. Each platform may have specific file format, size, and resolution requirements. Familiarize yourself with these specifications to ensure that your artwork meets the necessary criteria for minting and selling as an NFT.

4.4.2.4 Metadata and Tokenization

NFTs are not just about the visual artwork; they also include metadata that provides additional information about the asset. This metadata can include details such as the artist's name, description, creation date, and even unlockable content. Consider how you can enhance the value of your NFT by adding meaningful metadata that adds to the overall experience for the collector.

4.4.2.5 Rarity and Scarcity

Creating scarcity and rarity can significantly impact the value of your NFT. Consider releasing limited editions or creating unique variations of your artwork. This can be achieved by creating different versions, adding unlockable content, or even collaborating with other artists. By making your NFTs scarce, you can increase their desirability and potentially command higher prices in the marketplace.

4.4.3 Tools for Designing NFTs

To design NFTs, you'll need access to various tools and software. Here are some popular tools that can help you create stunning NFTs:

4.4.3.1 Graphic Design Software

Graphic design software such as Adobe Photoshop, Illustrator, or Procreate can be used to create and manipulate digital artwork. These tools provide a wide range of features and capabilities to bring your creative vision to life.

4.4.3.2 3D Modeling Software

If you're interested in creating 3D NFTs or virtual reality experiences, 3D modeling software like Blender or Maya can be invaluable. These tools allow you to create intricate 3D models, textures, and animations that can be exported as NFTs.

4.4.3.3 Digital Art Marketplaces

To mint and sell your NFTs, you'll need to choose a digital art marketplace that supports NFTs. Some popular platforms include OpenSea, Rarible, SuperRare, and Foundation. Each platform has its own set of features, fees, and community, so it's important to research and choose the one that aligns with your goals as an artist.

4.4.4 Promoting and Selling NFTs

Designing NFTs is just the first step; promoting and selling them is equally important. Here are some strategies to consider:

4.4.4.1 Building an Online Presence

Establishing an online presence is crucial for promoting your NFTs. Create a website or portfolio to showcase your artwork and provide information about your NFTs. Utilize social media platforms like Twitter, Instagram, and Discord to engage with the NFT community, share your work, and connect with potential buyers.

4.4.4.2 Collaborations and Partnerships

Collaborating with other artists or partnering with established NFT collectors can help increase the visibility and reach of your NFTs. Consider joining communities or participating in events where you can connect with like-minded individuals and explore collaboration opportunities.

4.4.4.3 Engaging with the NFT Community

Engaging with the NFT community is essential for building a network of supporters and potential buyers. Participate in discussions, attend virtual events, and contribute to the community by sharing your knowledge and experiences. By actively engaging with the community, you can gain valuable insights, feedback, and exposure for your NFTs.

Conclusion

Designing NFTs and digital art is an exciting and rapidly evolving field within Web3. By understanding the fundamentals of NFTs, honing your artistic skills, and leveraging the right tools and platforms, you can create compelling and valuable digital assets. Remember to stay connected with the NFT community, continuously learn and adapt to emerging trends, and embrace the opportunities that Web3 presents for digital designers.

5 Web3 Design Best Practices

5.1 Accessibility and Inclusive Design

In the world of digital design, it is essential to create experiences that are accessible and inclusive for all users. Accessibility refers to the practice of designing and developing websites, applications, and other digital products in a way that allows people with disabilities to perceive, understand, navigate, and interact with them effectively. Inclusive design, on the other hand, goes beyond accessibility and aims to create products that can be used by as many people as possible, regardless of their abilities, age, gender, or cultural background.

5.1.1 Understanding Accessibility

Accessibility is not just a legal requirement but also a moral and ethical responsibility for digital designers. By making your designs accessible, you ensure that everyone, including people with disabilities, can access and use your products. This includes individuals with visual impairments, hearing impairments, motor disabilities, cognitive disabilities, and other disabilities.

To create accessible designs, it is crucial to understand the different types of disabilities and how they can impact user interactions. For example, individuals with visual impairments may rely on screen readers or magnification tools to access content, while those with hearing impairments may require captions or transcripts for audio and video content. Motor disabilities may affect a person's ability to use a mouse or keyboard, requiring alternative input methods such as voice commands or keyboard shortcuts.

5.1.2 Designing for Accessibility

Designing for accessibility involves considering various factors throughout the design process. Here are some key considerations:

5.1.2.1 Color Contrast

Ensure that there is sufficient contrast between text and background colors to make it easy for users with visual impairments to read the content. Use tools like color contrast checkers to verify the contrast ratio meets accessibility standards.

5.1.2.2 Text Alternatives

Provide alternative text descriptions for images, icons, and other non-text elements. This allows screen readers to convey the information to users who cannot see the visual content.

5.1.2.3 Clear and Consistent Navigation

Create clear and consistent navigation structures to help users understand and navigate through your website or application. Use descriptive link text and provide skip navigation options for users who rely on keyboard navigation.

5.1.2.4 Keyboard Accessibility

Ensure that all interactive elements, such as buttons and form fields, can be accessed and operated using a keyboard alone. This is crucial for users who cannot use a mouse or other pointing devices.

5.1.2.5 Captions and Transcripts

Include captions or transcripts for audio and video content to make it accessible to users with hearing impairments. This allows them to understand the content even if they cannot hear the audio.

5.1.2.6 Responsive Design

Design your websites and applications to be responsive, adapting to different screen sizes and devices. This ensures that users can access and interact with your content regardless of the device they are using.

5.1.3 Inclusive Design Principles

Inclusive design goes beyond accessibility and aims to create products that are usable and enjoyable for a diverse range of users. Here are some principles to consider when designing inclusively:

5.1.3.1 Diversity and Representation

Consider the diverse needs and perspectives of your users when designing. Represent different cultures, genders, ages, and abilities in your design choices to ensure that your product is inclusive and relatable to a wide range of users.

5.1.3.2 Flexibility and Customization

Provide options for users to customize the interface according to their preferences and needs. This could include adjustable font sizes, color themes, or alternative input methods.

5.1.3.3 Clear and Concise Language

Use clear and concise language in your designs to ensure that the content is easily understandable by all users, regardless of their language proficiency or cognitive abilities.

5.1.3.4 User Testing and Feedback

Involve users with diverse backgrounds and abilities in the design process. Conduct user testing and gather feedback to identify any usability issues and make necessary improvements to enhance inclusivity.

5.1.4 Tools and Resources

There are several tools and resources available to assist digital designers in creating accessible and inclusive designs. Here are a few examples:

- **Screen Readers**: Tools like NVDA, JAWS, and VoiceOver simulate the experience of visually impaired users and help designers understand how their designs are perceived by screen reader users.
- **Color Contrast Checkers**: Online tools like WebAIM's Color Contrast Checker or Contrast Ratio provide a quick way to check the contrast ratio between text and background colors.
- **Accessibility Guidelines**: Familiarize yourself with accessibility guidelines such as the Web Content Accessibility Guidelines (WCAG) to understand the best practices and requirements for creating accessible designs.
- **User Testing Platforms**: Platforms like UserTesting or UserZoom allow you to recruit participants with diverse backgrounds and abilities to conduct usability testing and gather feedback on your designs.

- **Inclusive Design Resources:** Explore resources like the Inclusive Design Toolkit by the University of Cambridge or the Inclusive Design Principles by the Inclusive Design Research Centre for more guidance on inclusive design practices.

By incorporating accessibility and inclusive design principles into your work, you can create digital experiences that are accessible to all users, regardless of their abilities or backgrounds. This not only ensures compliance with legal requirements but also enhances the usability and inclusivity of your designs, making them more impactful and meaningful to a wider audience.

5.2 Responsive and Adaptive Design

In today's digital landscape, where users access websites and applications from a variety of devices with different screen sizes and resolutions, it is crucial for digital designers to create designs that are responsive and adaptive. Responsive and adaptive design ensures that the user experience remains consistent and optimal across all devices, whether it's a desktop computer, a tablet, or a smartphone. In this section, we will explore the principles and best practices of responsive and adaptive design in the context of Web3.

5.2.1 Understanding Responsive Design

Responsive design is an approach to web design that aims to create websites and applications that automatically adjust and adapt to the user's device and screen size. It involves designing and developing flexible layouts, fluid images, and scalable typography that can seamlessly resize and reposition themselves based on the screen dimensions.

To achieve responsive design, digital designers need to consider a few key principles:

Fluid Grids:

A fluid grid system allows the layout to adapt to different screen sizes by using relative units such as percentages instead of fixed pixel values. This ensures that the content can be displayed in a flexible and fluid manner, regardless of the device being used.

Flexible Images:

Images play a crucial role in web design, and they need to be optimized for different screen sizes. Using CSS techniques such as max-width: 100% ensures that images scale proportionally and do not overflow or become distorted on smaller screens.

Media Queries:

Media queries are CSS rules that allow designers to apply different styles based on the characteristics of the user's device, such as screen size, resolution, and orientation. By using media queries, designers can create breakpoints at which the layout and design elements can adapt to provide the best user experience.

Mobile-First Approach:

With the increasing dominance of mobile devices, adopting a mobile-first approach has become essential. This approach involves designing for mobile devices first and then progressively enhancing the design for larger screens. By starting with the smallest screen size, designers can prioritize the most important content and ensure a smooth experience on all devices.

5.2.2 Adaptive Design for Web3

While responsive design focuses on adapting the layout and content to different screen sizes, adaptive design takes it a step further by considering the specific capabilities and features of the user's device. In the context of Web3, adaptive design becomes even more important as it involves designing for various blockchain-enabled devices and interfaces.

Device-Specific Considerations:

Web3 applications can be accessed through a range of devices, including desktop computers, smartphones, tablets, and even hardware wallets. Each device has its own unique capabilities and limitations. For example, a hardware wallet may have a small screen and limited input options, while a desktop computer may have a larger screen and more processing power. Designers need to consider these factors and create adaptive designs that cater to the specific needs of each device.

Blockchain Interface Design:

Web3 applications often involve interacting with blockchain networks and decentralized protocols. Designers need to consider the complexities of blockchain interactions and design intuitive interfaces that guide users through the process. This may involve visualizing transaction confirmations, displaying wallet balances, or providing clear instructions for interacting with smart contracts.

Performance Optimization:

In the Web3 world, where transactions and interactions happen on the blockchain, performance optimization becomes crucial. Slow-loading websites and applications can lead to a poor user experience and frustration. Designers need to optimize assets, minimize network requests, and prioritize critical content to ensure fast and efficient loading times.

Dark Mode and Accessibility:

With the increasing popularity of dark mode, designers should consider implementing this feature in their Web3 designs. Dark mode not only provides a visually appealing alternative but also helps reduce eye strain and save battery life on certain devices. Additionally, designers should ensure that their designs are accessible to users with disabilities by following accessibility guidelines and providing alternative text for images, proper color contrast, and keyboard navigation options.

5.2.3 Tools and Frameworks for Responsive and Adaptive Design

To facilitate the creation of responsive and adaptive designs, there are several tools and frameworks available that can streamline the design and development process. Some popular ones include:

CSS Frameworks:

CSS frameworks like Bootstrap, Foundation, and Bulma provide pre-built responsive grid systems, components, and styles that can be easily customized and integrated into web projects. These frameworks offer a solid foundation for creating responsive designs without starting from scratch.

CSS Preprocessors:

CSS preprocessors like Sass and Less enable designers to write more maintainable and modular CSS code. They offer features such as variables, mixins, and functions that can be used to create reusable styles and streamline the development process.

Design and Prototyping Tools:

Design tools like Figma, Sketch, and Adobe XD provide features specifically designed for creating responsive and adaptive designs. These tools allow designers to create artboards for different screen sizes, define breakpoints, and preview designs on various devices.

Testing and Debugging Tools:

Testing and debugging tools like browser developer tools and online emulators help designers identify and fix issues related to responsive and adaptive design. These tools allow designers to simulate different screen sizes and orientations, inspect element properties, and test the responsiveness of their designs.

Conclusion

Responsive and adaptive design is essential for creating user-friendly and accessible Web3 experiences. By considering the principles and best practices outlined in this section, digital designers can ensure that their designs are optimized for different devices, screen sizes, and capabilities. With the right tools and frameworks, designers can streamline the design and development process and create engaging and adaptive designs that cater to the evolving world of Web3.

5.3 Designing for Performance and Speed

In the fast-paced world of the internet, performance and speed are crucial factors that can make or break a website or application. Users have become increasingly impatient, expecting websites to load quickly and respond instantaneously to their interactions. As a digital designer venturing into the world of Web3, it is essential to understand the importance of designing for performance and speed to provide users with a seamless and efficient experience.

5.3.1 Optimizing Images and Media

One of the primary culprits for slow-loading websites is the improper handling of images and media. High-resolution images and large media files can significantly impact the loading time of a webpage. To ensure optimal performance, it is crucial to optimize images and media files before incorporating them into your designs.

There are several techniques you can employ to optimize images. Firstly, you can compress images without compromising their quality using tools like Adobe Photoshop, Squoosh, or TinyPNG. By reducing the file size of images, you can significantly improve loading times. Additionally, consider using responsive images that adapt to different screen sizes, ensuring that users only download the necessary image data.

When it comes to media files, such as videos and audio, consider using formats that offer better compression, such as WebM or MP4 for videos and AAC for audio. Furthermore, lazy loading techniques can be employed to defer the loading of media files until they are needed, reducing the initial load time of a webpage.

5.3.2 Minifying and Bundling Code

Another crucial aspect of designing for performance and speed is optimizing the code that powers your website or application. Minifying and bundling code can significantly reduce the file size and improve loading times.

Minification involves removing unnecessary characters, such as whitespace and comments, from your code without altering its functionality. This process reduces the file size, making it quicker to download and parse. There are various tools available, such as

UglifyJS and Terser, that can automatically minify your JavaScript code.

Bundling code involves combining multiple files into a single file, reducing the number of HTTP requests required to load a webpage. This technique is particularly useful when working with JavaScript frameworks or libraries that consist of multiple files. Tools like Webpack and Rollup can help you bundle your code efficiently.

5.3.3 Caching and Content Delivery Networks (CDNs)

Caching is a technique that involves storing frequently accessed data, such as images, scripts, and stylesheets, in the user's browser or on a server. By caching static assets, you can reduce the number of requests made to the server, resulting in faster loading times.

When implementing caching, it is essential to set appropriate cache headers to control how long the assets should be cached. You can use techniques like versioning or cache busting to ensure that users receive the latest version of your assets when updates are made.

Content Delivery Networks (CDNs) can also significantly improve the performance of your website or application. CDNs are distributed networks of servers located in various geographical locations. When a user requests a resource, the CDN serves it from the server closest to the user, reducing latency and improving loading times. Consider utilizing a CDN to deliver your static assets, such as images, scripts, and stylesheets, for optimal performance.

5.3.4 Optimizing Web Fonts

Web fonts can enhance the visual appeal of a website or application, but they can also impact performance if not optimized correctly. When using web fonts, it is crucial to strike a balance between aesthetics and performance.

To optimize web fonts, consider using font subsets that include only the characters required for your content. This reduces the file size of the font, resulting in faster loading times. Additionally, utilize font loading techniques, such as the "font-display" property, to control how the font is rendered while it is loading. This ensures that users see content even if the font hasn't finished loading, preventing a flash of unstyled text (FOUT) or invisible text.

5.3.5 Mobile Optimization

With the increasing use of mobile devices, optimizing your designs for mobile performance is paramount. Mobile optimization involves designing and developing websites and applications that load quickly and provide a seamless experience on mobile devices.

To optimize for mobile performance, consider implementing responsive design techniques. Responsive design allows your website or application to adapt to different screen sizes and resolutions, ensuring that users on mobile devices have a smooth and efficient experience. Additionally, prioritize the use of lightweight frameworks and libraries that are optimized for mobile performance.

Furthermore, consider implementing progressive web app (PWA) features to enhance the performance of your web applications on mobile devices. PWAs allow users to install your web application on their home screens, providing a native-like experience with offline capabilities and faster loading times.

5.3.6 Continuous Performance Monitoring

Designing for performance and speed is an ongoing process. It is crucial to continuously monitor and optimize the performance of your website or application to ensure a smooth user experience.

There are various tools available, such as Google PageSpeed Insights, Lighthouse, and WebPageTest, that can help you analyze and identify performance bottlenecks. These tools provide insights into areas that require improvement, such as image optimization, code minification, and caching.

Regularly monitoring your website or application's performance allows you to identify and address any issues promptly, ensuring that your designs remain fast and efficient.

By incorporating these best practices into your Web3 designs, you can create high-performing and fast-loading experiences for your users. Remember, performance and speed are crucial factors that contribute to user satisfaction and engagement, making them essential considerations in the world of Web3 design.

5.4 Security and Privacy Considerations

In the world of Web3 design, security and privacy considerations play a crucial role in ensuring the safety and protection of users' data and assets. As a digital designer, it is essential to understand the potential risks and vulnerabilities that exist in the Web3 ecosystem and implement best practices to mitigate them. This section will explore some key security and privacy considerations that every Web3 designer should be aware of.

5.4.1 Secure Authentication and Authorization

One of the primary concerns in Web3 design is ensuring secure authentication and authorization mechanisms. Traditional username and password-based authentication may not be sufficient in the decentralized Web3 environment. Instead, designers should explore more robust authentication methods such as decentralized identity (DID) systems, multi-factor authentication (MFA), or biometric authentication. These methods provide an extra layer of security and protect users' accounts from unauthorized access.

When designing authentication interfaces, it is crucial to prioritize user experience while maintaining security. Clear and intuitive instructions should be provided to guide users through the authentication process. Additionally, designers should consider incorporating visual cues, such as lock icons or color indicators, to reassure users about the security of their interactions.

5.4.2 Data Encryption and Storage

Web3 applications often deal with sensitive user data, such as private keys, wallet addresses, or personal information. Designers must ensure that this data is encrypted and stored securely to prevent unauthorized access or data breaches. Encryption algorithms like

AES (Advanced Encryption Standard) or RSA (Rivest-Shamir-Adleman) can be used to protect sensitive data both in transit and at rest.

When designing interfaces that involve data input or storage, designers should consider implementing end-to-end encryption to ensure that data remains encrypted throughout its lifecycle. Additionally, it is essential to educate users about the importance of data security and provide clear instructions on how to protect their own data, such as using hardware wallets or secure password management tools.

5.4.3 User Privacy and Consent

Respecting user privacy and obtaining explicit consent for data collection and usage is a fundamental principle of Web3 design. Designers should be transparent about the data being collected, how it will be used, and provide users with granular control over their privacy settings. This can be achieved through clear and concise privacy policies, cookie consent banners, and user-friendly privacy settings interfaces.

To enhance user trust, designers should adopt privacy by design principles, which involve integrating privacy considerations into the design process from the very beginning. This includes minimizing data collection, anonymizing data whenever possible, and regularly reviewing and updating privacy practices to align with evolving regulations and best practices.

5.4.4 Secure Transactions and Smart Contracts

Web3 applications often involve financial transactions and interactions with smart contracts. Designers should prioritize the security of these transactions to protect users' funds and assets. When designing transaction interfaces, it is crucial to provide clear and accurate information about the transaction, including recipient addresses, transaction fees, and gas limits.

To prevent phishing attacks and ensure the integrity of transactions, designers should consider implementing visual indicators, such as verified addresses or transaction confirmations, to help users verify the authenticity of the transaction. Additionally, designers should educate users about common security risks, such as the importance of double-checking addresses and avoiding suspicious links or attachments.

5.4.5 Regular Security Audits and Updates

Web3 technologies and frameworks are continuously evolving, and new security vulnerabilities may emerge over time. It is essential for designers to stay updated with the latest security best practices and conduct regular security audits of their designs and applications. This can involve collaborating with security experts or conducting penetration testing to identify and address any potential vulnerabilities.

Furthermore, designers should actively monitor security advisories and updates from Web3 frameworks and libraries they use in their designs. Promptly applying security patches and updates is crucial to ensure the ongoing security of Web3 applications.

5.4.6 User Education and Support

Designers have a responsibility to educate users about security best practices and provide support in case of security-related issues. This can be achieved through clear and concise documentation, tutorials, and FAQs that address common security concerns and provide step-by-step instructions on how to secure user accounts and assets.

Additionally, designers should consider incorporating in-app support features, such as live chat or support tickets, to assist users in resolving security-related queries or reporting suspicious activities. By empowering users with knowledge and support, designers can contribute to a safer and more secure Web3 ecosystem.

In conclusion, security and privacy considerations are paramount in Web3 design. By implementing secure authentication and authorization mechanisms, encrypting and storing data securely, respecting user privacy and consent, ensuring secure transactions and smart contracts, conducting regular security audits, and providing user education and support, designers can contribute to a more secure and trustworthy Web3 experience for users.

6 Collaboration and Workflow in Web3 Design

6.1 Working with Developers and Blockchain Experts

Collaboration is a crucial aspect of web3 design, as it requires a multidisciplinary approach that combines the skills of digital designers, developers, and blockchain experts. In this section, we will explore the importance of working closely with developers and blockchain experts and how to establish effective collaboration and workflow in web3 design projects.

6.1.1 Understanding the Roles and Responsibilities

To effectively collaborate with developers and blockchain experts, it is essential to understand their roles and responsibilities. Digital designers are responsible for creating visually appealing and user-friendly interfaces, while developers focus on implementing the functionality and technical aspects of the design. Blockchain experts bring their knowledge of blockchain technology and its implications for design and user experience.

Digital designers should have a basic understanding of coding languages such as HTML, CSS, and JavaScript to communicate effectively with developers. Similarly, developers should have a basic understanding of design principles and user experience to ensure the implementation aligns with the intended design.

6.1.2 Establishing Effective Communication

Clear and effective communication is the foundation of successful collaboration. When working with developers and blockchain experts, it is crucial to establish open lines of communication and maintain regular contact throughout the project.

Regular meetings, either in person or through video conferencing, can help align everyone's understanding of the project goals, design requirements, and technical constraints. It is essential to encourage open dialogue, ask questions, and address any concerns or challenges that may arise.

Using collaboration tools such as project management software, communication platforms, and version control systems can streamline communication and ensure everyone is on the same page. These tools allow for real-time updates, document sharing, and easy tracking of progress.

6.1.3 Embracing an Agile Workflow

Adopting an agile workflow can greatly enhance collaboration between digital designers, developers, and blockchain experts. Agile methodologies, such as Scrum or Kanban, promote iterative development, continuous feedback, and flexibility in adapting to changing requirements.

In an agile workflow, the project is divided into smaller tasks or user stories, which are then prioritized and assigned to the respective team members. Regular sprints or iterations allow for frequent feedback and course correction, ensuring that the design and development processes remain aligned.

By embracing an agile workflow, digital designers can work closely with developers and blockchain experts, providing continuous feedback on the implementation and making necessary design adjustments along the way. This iterative approach fosters collaboration, reduces the risk of misunderstandings, and allows for faster and more efficient project delivery.

6.1.4 Leveraging Design Systems and Component Libraries

Design systems and component libraries play a vital role in streamlining collaboration between digital designers and developers. A design system is a collection of reusable components, guidelines, and design principles that ensure consistency and efficiency in the design process.

By using a design system, digital designers can create a library of pre-designed components that developers can easily implement. This not only saves time but also ensures consistency across different parts of the application or website.

Collaboration between digital designers and developers is further enhanced by establishing a shared language and understanding of the design system. Regular communication and feedback help refine the design system, making it more effective and adaptable to the project's needs.

6.1.5 Emphasizing Testing and Quality Assurance

Collaboration between digital designers, developers, and blockchain experts should also extend to testing and quality assurance. Thorough testing ensures that the design is implemented correctly, and the functionality works as intended.

Digital designers can collaborate with developers to conduct user testing, identify any usability issues, and make necessary design adjustments. Similarly, blockchain experts can help test the integration of blockchain technology and ensure its smooth functioning within the design.

By emphasizing testing and quality assurance, collaboration becomes a continuous process of improvement and refinement. Regular feedback loops and bug tracking systems can help address any issues promptly, ensuring a high-quality end product.

6.1.6 Continuous Learning and Growth

The world of web3 design is constantly evolving, and collaboration with developers and blockchain experts provides an opportunity for continuous learning and growth. By working closely with these professionals, digital designers can gain insights into the technical aspects of web3 and expand their skill set.

Attending workshops, conferences, and online courses related to blockchain technology and development can deepen the understanding of the underlying technologies and their impact on design. Engaging in discussions and knowledge sharing within the web3 community can also foster collaboration and open up new opportunities for learning.

Collaboration with developers and blockchain experts not only enhances the design process but also broadens the perspective of digital designers, enabling them to create innovative and impactful web3 experiences.

In conclusion, collaboration with developers and blockchain experts is essential for successful web3 design projects. By understanding each other's roles and responsibilities, establishing effective communication, embracing an agile workflow, leveraging design systems, emphasizing testing and quality assurance, and fostering continuous learning, digital designers can enter the world of web3 and create exceptional experiences that integrate design, technology, and blockchain seamlessly.

6.2 Design Systems and Component Libraries

Design systems and component libraries play a crucial role in the world of web3 design. They provide a structured approach to designing and building user interfaces, ensuring consistency, efficiency, and scalability. In this section, we will explore the importance of design systems and component libraries in web3 design and discuss how you can create and implement them effectively.

6.2.1 Understanding Design Systems

A design system is a collection of reusable components, guidelines, and assets that help maintain consistency and coherence across a product or platform. It serves as a single source of truth for design decisions, ensuring that all elements of a user interface align with the overall brand identity and user experience.

In the context of web3 design, a design system becomes even more critical due to the decentralized nature of blockchain applications. With multiple developers and designers working on different aspects of a project, a design system acts as a central repository of design principles, patterns, and components. It enables teams to collaborate effectively and ensures a cohesive user experience across various decentralized applications (DApps) and interfaces.

6.2.2 Benefits of Design Systems in Web3 Design

Implementing a design system in web3 design offers several benefits:

Consistency and Efficiency

A design system establishes a set of standardized components, styles, and patterns that can be reused across different projects. This consistency not only enhances the user experience but also saves time and effort for designers and developers. By reusing pre-designed components, teams can focus on solving unique design challenges rather than reinventing the wheel for every project.

Scalability and Flexibility

As the web3 ecosystem continues to evolve, new DApps and interfaces are constantly being developed. A design system provides a scalable framework that can adapt to changing requirements and accommodate future growth. By designing components that are modular and flexible, teams can easily update and extend the system as new features and functionalities are introduced.

Brand Identity and User Experience

A design system ensures that all elements of a user interface align with the brand identity and user experience goals. By defining a consistent visual language, typography, color palette, and interaction patterns, teams can create a cohesive and recognizable brand presence. This consistency builds trust and familiarity among users, enhancing their overall experience with the product or platform.

Collaboration and Communication

Design systems act as a common language between designers, developers, and other stakeholders involved in a web3 project. They provide a shared understanding of design principles and guidelines, facilitating effective collaboration and communication. With a design system in place, teams can work together seamlessly, reducing misunderstandings and ensuring that everyone is aligned with the project's vision.

6.2.3 Creating a Design System

Creating a design system requires careful planning and collaboration. Here are some steps to help you get started:

Define Design Principles

Start by defining the design principles that will guide your system. These principles should align with the brand identity and user experience goals of your project. Consider factors such as simplicity, accessibility, and scalability when formulating these principles.

Identify and Document Components

Identify the common components that will be used across your web3 project. These may include buttons, forms, navigation menus, and other UI elements. Document each component's purpose, behavior, and variations. Use visual examples and code snippets to illustrate how each component should be implemented.

Establish Design Guidelines

Establish design guidelines that cover typography, color palette, spacing, and other visual aspects. Define the rules for using these elements consistently throughout your project. Consider accessibility guidelines and ensure that your design system is inclusive and usable by a wide range of users.

Build a Component Library

Create a component library that houses all the reusable components defined in your design system. This library can be a collection of code snippets, design files, or a combination of both. Ensure that the library is easily accessible and well-documented, allowing designers and developers to find and implement components efficiently.

Test and Iterate

Regularly test and iterate on your design system to ensure its effectiveness. Gather feedback from designers, developers, and users to identify areas for improvement. Continuously update and refine your design system based on these insights, keeping it up to date with the evolving needs of your web3 project.

6.2.4 Implementing a Design System

Implementing a design system involves integrating it into your design and development workflow. Here are some key considerations:

Training and Onboarding

Ensure that all team members are familiar with the design system and understand how to use it effectively. Provide training and onboarding sessions to introduce the system and its components. Encourage collaboration and knowledge sharing among team members to foster a culture of using the design system consistently.

Version Control and Documentation

Use version control systems to manage changes and updates to your design system. This allows you to track revisions, roll back changes if necessary, and maintain a history of the system's evolution. Additionally, document the design system thoroughly, including guidelines, component usage, and any updates or changes made over time.

Integration with Design Tools and Development Frameworks

Integrate your design system with popular design tools and development frameworks to streamline the design and development process. This integration ensures that designers and developers have easy access to the components and guidelines defined in the system. It also promotes consistency and reduces the chances of errors or inconsistencies during implementation.

Collaboration and Feedback

Encourage collaboration and feedback from all stakeholders involved in the web3 project. Regularly review and update the design system based on user feedback, design critiques, and technological advancements. This iterative approach ensures that the design system remains relevant and effective throughout the project's lifecycle.

Conclusion

Design systems and component libraries are essential tools for web3 designers. They provide a structured approach to designing and building user interfaces, ensuring consistency, efficiency, and scalability. By creating and implementing a design system, you can streamline collaboration, maintain brand identity, and deliver exceptional user experiences in the decentralized world of web3 design.

6.3 Testing and Iteration in Web3 Design

Testing and iteration are crucial aspects of the design process in any field, and web3 design is no exception. In this section, we will explore the importance of testing and iteration in web3 design and discuss some best practices to ensure the success of your designs.

6.3.1 The Importance of Testing in Web3 Design

Testing is an essential step in the web3 design process as it allows you to evaluate the usability, functionality, and overall user experience of your designs. By conducting thorough testing, you can identify any issues or areas for improvement before launching your web3 project.

In web3 design, testing takes on a unique significance due to the decentralized nature of blockchain technology and the potential impact it can have on user interactions. It is crucial to ensure that your designs are not only visually appealing but also functional and secure.

6.3.2 User Testing in Web3 Design

User testing plays a vital role in web3 design as it allows you to gather feedback directly from your target audience. By observing how users interact with your designs, you can gain valuable insights into their needs, preferences, and pain points. This information can then be used to refine and iterate on your designs.

When conducting user testing in web3 design, it is essential to consider the unique aspects of blockchain technology. For example, you may need to test how users interact with decentralized applications (DApps) or navigate through blockchain-based interfaces. By simulating real-world scenarios and observing user behavior, you can identify any usability issues and make necessary improvements.

6.3.3 A/B Testing in Web3 Design

A/B testing is a powerful technique that allows you to compare two or more versions of a design to determine which one performs better. In web3 design, A/B testing can be used to test different user interfaces, layouts, or even blockchain interactions.

To conduct A/B testing in web3 design, you can create multiple variations of your design and randomly assign users to each version. By measuring key metrics such as user engagement, conversion rates, or transaction completion, you can determine which design performs better and make data-driven decisions.

6.3.4 Security Testing in Web3 Design

Security is a critical consideration in web3 design, given the decentralized and immutable nature of blockchain technology. Conducting thorough security testing is essential to identify any vulnerabilities or weaknesses in your designs that could be exploited by malicious actors.

In web3 design, security testing involves assessing the robustness of your designs against potential threats such as hacking attempts, data breaches, or smart contract vulnerabilities. This can be done through techniques such as penetration testing, code reviews, or vulnerability scanning. By addressing any security issues early on, you can ensure the integrity and trustworthiness of your web3 project.

6.3.5 Iteration and Continuous Improvement

Iteration is a fundamental aspect of the design process in web3. By continuously iterating on your designs based on user feedback and testing results, you can refine and improve the overall user experience.

In web3 design, iteration involves making incremental changes to your designs based on the insights gained from testing. This could include refining the user interface, optimizing performance, or enhancing security measures. By embracing an iterative approach, you can create designs that are not only visually appealing but also functional, user-friendly, and aligned with the principles of web3.

6.3.6 Best Practices for Testing and Iteration in Web3 Design

To ensure effective testing and iteration in web3 design, consider the following best practices:

1. Start testing early: Begin testing your designs as early as possible in the design process to identify and address any issues before they become more challenging to fix.
2. Test with real users: Conduct user testing with your target audience to gain valuable insights into their needs, preferences, and pain points.
3. Embrace A/B testing: Use A/B testing to compare different versions of your designs and make data-driven decisions.
4. Prioritize security testing: Conduct thorough security testing to identify and address any vulnerabilities or weaknesses in your designs.

5. Iterate based on feedback: Continuously iterate on your designs based on user feedback and testing results to improve the overall user experience.
6. Document and track changes: Keep a record of the changes made during the iteration process to ensure transparency and facilitate collaboration with other team members.
7. Stay up to date with web3 trends: Stay informed about the latest trends and developments in web3 design to ensure your designs are innovative and aligned with industry standards.

By following these best practices, you can ensure that your web3 designs are user-friendly, secure, and optimized for the decentralized nature of blockchain technology.

In the next chapter, we will explore the importance of marketing and branding in web3 and discuss strategies to promote your web3 projects effectively.

7 Marketing and Branding in Web3

7.1 Community Building and Engagement

Building a strong community and fostering engagement is crucial for the success of any web3 project. In the rapidly evolving landscape of web3, community plays a vital role in driving adoption, creating a network effect, and establishing trust among users. As a digital designer looking to enter the world of web3, understanding how to build and engage with a community is essential. This section will explore the strategies and best practices for community building and engagement in the context of web3.

7.1.1 Understanding the Importance of Community

In the web3 ecosystem, community is not just a group of users, but a network of individuals who share a common interest and belief in the project's vision. A strong community can provide valuable feedback, contribute to the project's development, and act as advocates, spreading the word about the project to a wider audience. Moreover, a vibrant community can attract investors, partners, and collaborators, leading to the growth and sustainability of the project.

7.1.2 Defining Your Target Audience

Before diving into community building, it is essential to define your target audience. Understanding who your users are and what they value will help you tailor your messaging and engagement strategies. Conduct market research to identify the demographics, interests, and pain points of your target audience. This information will guide your design decisions and enable you to create experiences that resonate with your users.

7.1.3 Creating a Community Management Strategy

A well-defined community management strategy is the foundation for successful community building and engagement. Start by establishing clear goals and objectives for your community.

Determine what you want to achieve, whether it's increasing user adoption, fostering collaboration, or driving brand awareness.

Next, identify the platforms and channels where your target audience is most active. This could include social media platforms like Twitter, Discord, Telegram, or dedicated forums and discussion boards. Choose platforms that align with your project's values and where you can effectively engage with your community.

Develop a content strategy that provides value to your community. Share updates, tutorials, and educational content related to web3 and your project. Encourage community members to contribute their knowledge and insights, fostering a sense of ownership and collaboration.

Establish guidelines and moderation policies to ensure a safe and inclusive environment for your community. Encourage respectful and constructive discussions while discouraging spam and harmful behavior. Regularly monitor and moderate the community to maintain a positive atmosphere.

7.1.4 Engaging with Your Community

Engagement is a two-way street. Actively engaging with your community is essential to foster a sense of belonging and build trust. Here are some strategies to effectively engage with your community:

7.1.4.1 Regular Communication

Consistent and transparent communication is key to building trust and keeping your community informed. Regularly share updates, progress reports, and upcoming events. Be responsive to community feedback and address concerns promptly. Use newsletters, blog posts, and social media to keep your community engaged and informed.

7.1.4.2 Hosting Events and Workshops

Organize virtual events, webinars, and workshops to educate and engage your community. These events can range from technical deep dives to beginner-friendly tutorials. Encourage participation and provide opportunities for community members to ask questions and share their experiences. Consider hosting guest speakers and experts to provide diverse perspectives and insights.

7.1.4.3 Gamification and Incentives

Gamification can be a powerful tool to drive engagement and reward community participation. Consider implementing reward systems, badges, or token-based incentives to encourage active involvement. This can include activities such as contributing to the project's development, providing feedback, or referring new users. However, ensure that the incentives align with the project's goals and values.

7.1.4.4 Community Feedback and Collaboration

Actively seek feedback from your community and involve them in the decision-making process. Conduct surveys, polls, and user testing to gather insights and improve your product or service. Encourage community members to contribute ideas, suggestions, and bug reports. Consider establishing a community governance model that allows token holders or active community members to have a say in the project's direction.

7.1.4.5 Recognizing and Highlighting Community Contributions

Recognize and appreciate the contributions of your community members. Highlight their achievements, showcase their work, and give credit where it's due. This not only motivates community members to continue their involvement but also fosters a sense of pride and ownership.

7.1.5 Scaling and Nurturing Your Community

As your community grows, it becomes essential to scale your community management efforts. Consider appointing community managers or ambassadors who can help facilitate engagement, moderate discussions, and provide support. Empower your community members to become advocates and ambassadors for your project by providing them with the necessary resources and tools.

Nurturing your community requires ongoing effort and dedication. Continuously listen to your community's needs and adapt your strategies accordingly. Stay up to date with the latest trends and developments in the web3 space to provide relevant and valuable content. Regularly evaluate the success of your community engagement efforts and make adjustments as needed.

Conclusion

Community building and engagement are integral parts of the web3 ecosystem. As a digital designer entering the world of web3, understanding how to build and engage with a community is crucial for the success of your project. By defining your target audience, creating a community management strategy, and actively engaging with your community, you can foster a vibrant and supportive network that contributes to the growth and sustainability of your web3 project.

7.2 Marketing Strategies for Web3 Products

Marketing plays a crucial role in the success of any product or service, and the world of Web3 is no exception. As a digital designer venturing into the realm of Web3, it is essential to understand the unique marketing strategies that can help promote and grow your Web3 products. In this section, we will explore some effective marketing strategies specifically tailored for Web3 products.

7.2.1 Understanding the Web3 Audience

Before diving into marketing strategies, it is crucial to understand the target audience for your Web3 product. The Web3 space attracts a diverse range of users, including early adopters, crypto enthusiasts, developers, and investors. Each segment of the audience may have different motivations and interests, so it is essential to identify and understand your specific target audience.

To gain a deeper understanding of your audience, conduct market research, analyze user data, and engage with the Web3 community. This will help you tailor your marketing strategies to effectively reach and engage with your target audience.

7.2.2 Building a Strong Web3 Brand Identity

A strong brand identity is essential for any product or service, and it holds true for Web3 products as well. Your brand identity should reflect the values and vision of your Web3 project, creating a unique and memorable identity in the minds of your audience.

To build a strong brand identity, consider the following:

1. **Define your brand values:** Identify the core values that your Web3 project represents. This will help you create a brand identity that resonates with your target audience.
2. **Design a compelling brand logo and visual identity:** Create a visually appealing logo and design elements that align with your brand values. Consistency in visual elements across your website, social media, and marketing materials will help establish a strong brand presence.
3. **Craft a compelling brand story:** Develop a narrative that communicates the purpose and mission of your Web3 project. A compelling brand story can help create an emotional connection with your audience and differentiate your product from competitors.

4. **Engage with the Web3 community:** Actively participate in Web3 communities, forums, and social media platforms to build brand awareness and establish yourself as an authority in the space. Engage in discussions, share valuable insights, and contribute to the community to foster trust and credibility.

7.2.3 Content Strategy for Web3 Projects

Content marketing is a powerful tool for promoting Web3 products and educating the audience about the benefits and use cases of your product. A well-defined content strategy can help attract and engage users, build brand authority, and drive organic traffic to your website or platform.

Consider the following when developing a content strategy for your Web3 project:

1. **Identify relevant topics:** Research and identify topics that are relevant to your target audience and align with your Web3 project. This could include educational content about blockchain technology, tutorials on using your product, or thought leadership articles on the future of Web3.
2. **Create valuable and engaging content:** Develop high-quality content that provides value to your audience. This could include blog posts, whitepapers, case studies, videos, podcasts, or interactive content. Experiment with different formats to cater to different learning preferences.

3. **Optimize for search engines:** Implement SEO (Search Engine Optimization) techniques to ensure your content ranks well in search engine results. Use relevant keywords, optimize meta tags, and build backlinks to increase visibility and organic traffic to your website.
4. **Leverage social media:** Share your content on social media platforms to reach a wider audience. Engage with your followers, respond to comments, and encourage sharing to increase the reach and visibility of your content.
5. **Collaborate with influencers:** Identify influencers and thought leaders in the Web3 space who align with your brand values. Collaborate with them to create content, host webinars, or participate in interviews to leverage their audience and credibility.

7.2.4 Community Building and Engagement

Building a strong community around your Web3 project is crucial for its success. A vibrant and engaged community can help drive adoption, provide valuable feedback, and advocate for your product. Here are some strategies to build and engage with your Web3 community:

1. **Create a community platform:** Establish a dedicated community platform, such as a forum or Discord server, where users can connect, share ideas, and seek support. Encourage active participation and provide incentives for community members to contribute.

2. **Organize events and meetups:** Host virtual or physical events, webinars, or meetups to bring together your community members. These events can be educational, networking-focused, or product-focused, depending on your goals.

3. **Reward community participation:** Implement a reward system, such as token incentives or NFT giveaways, to encourage active participation and engagement within your community. This can help foster a sense of ownership and loyalty among community members.

4. **Listen and respond to feedback:** Actively listen to feedback from your community and respond promptly. Incorporate valuable suggestions and address concerns to show that you value the opinions of your community members.

5. **Collaborate with your community:** Involve your community in the decision-making process by seeking their input on new features, product updates, or marketing campaigns. This not only makes them feel valued but also increases their sense of ownership and commitment to your Web3 project.

7.2.5 Leveraging Influencer Marketing

Influencer marketing can be a powerful strategy to reach a wider audience and build credibility for your Web3 product. Identify influencers in the Web3 space who have a significant following and align with your brand values. Collaborate with them to promote your product, create sponsored content, or host giveaways.

When leveraging influencer marketing, consider the following:

1. **Relevance and authenticity:** Choose influencers whose audience aligns with your target audience and who have a genuine interest in Web3. Authenticity is key to building trust and credibility among the influencer's followers.

2. **Clear communication:** Clearly communicate your expectations, goals, and guidelines to the influencers you collaborate with. Ensure that they understand your product and its value proposition to effectively communicate it to their audience.

3. **Track and measure results:** Monitor the performance of influencer campaigns and track key metrics such as reach, engagement, and conversions. This will help you assess the effectiveness of your influencer marketing efforts and make data-driven decisions for future campaigns.

In conclusion, marketing strategies for Web3 products require a deep understanding of the target audience, a strong brand identity, a well-defined content strategy, active community engagement, and leveraging influencer marketing. By implementing these strategies, you can effectively promote your Web3 product, build a loyal user base, and drive adoption in the rapidly evolving world of Web3.

8 The Future of Web3 Design

8.1 Exploring Virtual Reality and Web3

Virtual reality (VR) has been a rapidly evolving technology that has captured the imagination of many. With the emergence of Web3, the integration of VR into the digital design landscape has become even more exciting. In this section, we will explore the intersection of virtual reality and Web3, and how digital designers can leverage this technology to create immersive and engaging experiences.

8.1.1 The Rise of Virtual Reality

Virtual reality refers to a simulated experience that can be similar to or completely different from the real world. It typically involves the use of a headset or other devices that create an immersive environment for the user. Over the years, VR has gained popularity in various industries, including gaming, entertainment, education, and even healthcare.

The advancements in VR technology have paved the way for more realistic and interactive experiences. With the introduction of Web3, the potential for integrating VR into web-based applications has expanded significantly. Web3 technologies, such as decentralized storage and blockchain, can enhance the capabilities of VR experiences by enabling secure and decentralized content distribution, ownership, and monetization.

8.1.2 Web3 and Virtual Reality

Web3, also known as the decentralized web, is a paradigm shift in the way we interact with the internet. It aims to create a more open, transparent, and user-centric online environment. By leveraging blockchain technology and decentralized protocols, Web3 enables peer-to-peer interactions, eliminates intermediaries, and empowers individuals to have greater control over their data and digital assets.

When combined with virtual reality, Web3 can revolutionize the way we experience and interact with digital content. VR experiences built on Web3 can offer users a more immersive and personalized journey. For example, users can explore virtual worlds, interact with digital objects, and even own virtual assets represented as non-fungible tokens (NFTs). These NFTs can be bought, sold, and traded on blockchain-powered marketplaces, providing a new dimension of ownership and value in the virtual realm.

8.1.3 Designing for Virtual Reality in Web3

Designing for virtual reality in the context of Web3 requires a deep understanding of both VR principles and Web3 technologies. Here are some key considerations for digital designers venturing into this exciting space:

8.1.3.1 User Experience and Interaction Design

Creating a seamless and intuitive user experience is crucial in VR design. As a digital designer, you need to consider how users will navigate and interact with the virtual environment. This includes designing intuitive user interfaces, defining clear interaction patterns, and ensuring smooth transitions between different VR scenes or elements.

8.1.3.2 Immersive Visual Design

Visual design plays a vital role in creating immersive VR experiences. You need to carefully consider factors such as color schemes, lighting, textures, and spatial arrangements to evoke the desired emotions and atmosphere. Additionally, optimizing visual assets for performance is crucial to ensure smooth rendering and minimize latency in VR environments.

8.1.3.3 Sound Design

Sound is an essential component of VR experiences as it enhances immersion and spatial awareness. Designers should pay attention to creating realistic and spatial audio cues that align with the virtual environment. This includes incorporating 3D audio techniques to simulate sound sources in different directions and distances, further enhancing the sense of presence in VR.

8.1.3.4 Integration with Web3 Technologies

To leverage the full potential of Web3 in VR design, digital designers need to understand how to integrate blockchain technology and decentralized protocols into their projects. This includes exploring the use of NFTs to represent virtual assets, leveraging decentralized storage solutions for hosting VR content, and integrating blockchain-based authentication and ownership verification mechanisms.

8.1.3.5 Performance Optimization

VR experiences require high-performance rendering to maintain a smooth and immersive user experience. Digital designers should optimize their assets and code to minimize latency and maximize frame rates. This includes optimizing 3D models, textures, and animations, as well as leveraging techniques like level of detail (LOD) rendering and occlusion culling to improve performance.

8.1.4 Challenges and Opportunities

While the integration of virtual reality and Web3 presents exciting opportunities, it also comes with its own set of challenges. Some of these challenges include the need for powerful hardware to run VR experiences, the complexity of designing for immersive environments, and the nascent nature of Web3 technologies.

However, the potential rewards are significant. By embracing virtual reality in the context of Web3, digital designers can create groundbreaking experiences that push the boundaries of traditional web design. They can explore new forms of storytelling, enable social interactions in virtual spaces, and empower users to truly own and shape their digital experiences.

8.1.5 Conclusion

Virtual reality and Web3 are two transformative technologies that have the potential to reshape the digital design landscape. By combining the immersive power of VR with the decentralized and user-centric nature of Web3, digital designers can create experiences that are not only visually stunning but also empower users to have greater control over their digital lives.

As a digital designer, embracing virtual reality and Web3 opens up a world of possibilities. By staying curious, experimenting with new tools and technologies, and continuously learning and adapting, you can position yourself at the forefront of this exciting intersection and become a pioneer in the future of Web3 design.

8.2 Conclusion: Becoming a Web3 Design Expert

Congratulations on completing this journey into the world of Web3 design! By now, you should have gained a solid understanding of the principles, technologies, and best practices that are essential for designing in the decentralized web. In this final section, we will explore the steps you can take to become a Web3 design expert and enter the exciting world of digital design.

8.2.1 Continual Learning and Skill Development

The field of digital design is constantly evolving, and staying up to date with the latest trends, technologies, and tools is crucial for success. As a Web3 design expert, you should embrace a mindset of continual learning and skill development. Here are some strategies to help you stay ahead:

1. Stay Informed: Follow industry blogs, newsletters, and social media accounts to stay updated on the latest Web3 design trends, news, and advancements. Engage in online communities and forums to connect with other designers and share knowledge.

2. Attend Workshops and Conferences: Participate in workshops, conferences, and meetups focused on Web3 design. These events provide opportunities to learn from

industry experts, network with like-minded professionals, and gain insights into emerging technologies.

3. Experiment and Explore: Set aside time for personal projects and experimentation. This allows you to explore new design techniques, tools, and concepts. Embrace a growth mindset and be open to trying new things.

4. Take Online Courses: Enroll in online courses or certifications that focus on Web3 design. Platforms like Coursera, Udemy, and LinkedIn Learning offer a wide range of courses taught by industry professionals.

8.2.2 Building a Strong Portfolio

A strong portfolio is essential for showcasing your skills and attracting potential clients or employers. As a Web3 design expert, your portfolio should demonstrate your expertise in designing for decentralized applications, blockchain interactions, NFTs, and other Web3 concepts. Here are some tips for building a compelling portfolio:

1. Showcase Diverse Projects: Include a variety of projects that highlight your versatility as a designer. This could include DApp interfaces, NFT designs, digital art, or any other Web3-related design work.

2. Explain Your Design Process: Provide insights into your design process for each project. Explain the problem you were trying to solve, the research you conducted, and the

design decisions you made. This helps potential clients or employers understand your approach and expertise.

3. Highlight Results and Impact: Whenever possible, include metrics or testimonials that demonstrate the impact of your design work. This could be increased user engagement, improved conversion rates, or positive feedback from users.
4. Keep it Updated: Regularly update your portfolio with your latest projects and skills. Remove outdated or irrelevant work to maintain a focused and relevant showcase of your abilities.

8.2.3 Networking and Collaboration

Networking and collaboration are essential for professional growth and opportunities in the Web3 design industry. Here are some strategies to help you build a strong network and collaborate with others:

1. Join Web3 Communities: Engage with Web3 communities on platforms like Discord, Telegram, and Reddit. Participate in discussions, share your knowledge, and connect with other designers, developers, and blockchain experts.
2. Attend Meetups and Conferences: Attend local meetups and conferences focused on Web3 design. These events provide opportunities to meet industry professionals, exchange ideas, and collaborate on projects.
3. Collaborate with Developers: Build relationships with developers and blockchain experts. Collaborating with them

on projects allows you to gain a deeper understanding of the technical aspects of Web3 and create more seamless and integrated designs.

4. Seek Mentorship: Find a mentor who is experienced in Web3 design. A mentor can provide guidance, support, and valuable insights as you navigate your career in this field.

8.2.4 Embracing the Future of Web3 Design

As a Web3 design expert, it is important to embrace the future of this rapidly evolving field. Here are some areas to keep an eye on:

1. Emerging Technologies: Stay updated on emerging technologies like virtual reality (VR), augmented reality (AR), and artificial intelligence (AI). These technologies have the potential to revolutionize the way we interact with the decentralized web.
2. Ethical Considerations: As Web3 design continues to evolve, ethical considerations become increasingly important. Stay informed about the ethical implications of your design decisions and strive to create inclusive, accessible, and user-centric experiences.
3. Cross-disciplinary Collaboration: Web3 design is a multidisciplinary field that requires collaboration with developers, blockchain experts, marketers, and other professionals. Embrace cross-disciplinary collaboration to create holistic and impactful designs.

4. User-Centric Design: Always prioritize the needs and expectations of your users. Conduct user research, gather feedback, and iterate on your designs to create intuitive and engaging experiences.

By following these strategies and embracing the future of Web3 design, you can position yourself as an expert in this exciting and rapidly growing field. Remember, the key to success lies in continual learning, building a strong portfolio, networking, and staying ahead of emerging trends. Good luck on your journey to becoming a Web3 design expert! This book ending is actually your beginning. It's what's in the middle that counts. Good Journey and go explore!

Made in the USA
Monee, IL
05 November 2026

67382715R00081